LIVING YOUR STRENGTHS

Discover your God-given talents
and inspire your community

CATHOLIC EDITION

Albert L. Winseman, D.Min.
Donald O. Clifton, Ph.D.
Curt Liesveld, M.Div.

Gallup Press
1251 Avenue of the Americas
23rd Floor
New York, NY 10020

Manufactured in the United States of America

Second edition 2008

10 9 8 7 6 5 4 3

Library of Congress Control Number: 2008928341

ISBN: 978-1-59562-022-4

For my wife Jane:
You are and always will be
the love of my life and my greatest source of strength.
—Albert L. Winseman

To Shirley, my wife of 57 years, who has helped our
four children live their strengths.
—Donald O. Clifton (1924 – 2003)

To my wife Rosanne:
Our marriage will always be my greatest success.
Your loving partnership continues to bring out the best of
what God has put in me.
—Curt Liesveld

We also dedicate this book to our coauthor, Don Clifton, who passed away in September 2003. Don's lifelong belief that people are at their best when they maximize their strengths, rather than try to fix their weaknesses, has inspired more than 3 million people to discover their talents and begin to live their strengths. We are deeply grateful to Don for the way he touched our lives.

—Al and Curt

TABLE OF CONTENTS

PREFACE TO THE SECOND EDITION

Five years ago, Gallup published the first edition of *Living Your Strengths*, a little paperback we thought would help introduce the strengths philosophy to faith communities. We had no grand marketing scheme, just the idea that we could better respond to inquiries about strengths with this book. Well, word got around, and it soon became apparent — as our supply of those paperbacks rapidly dwindled — that strengths development had struck a chord and that we would have to take further action to meet the growing demand.

That led to the hardback second edition in 2005, which, unlike the first edition, was available in bookstores. As sales grew and the demand spread, we published the Catholic Edition in 2006. Now, we are publishing our third edition, revised and expanded, also available as a Catholic Edition (This is the second edition of the Catholic *Living Your Strengths*). And, for the first time ever, both new editions are available in Spanish.

What we're witnessing is the progression of a movement — a movement with the power to transform the Church in all its varieties of expression. We're witnessing and experiencing the Strengths Movement, which is inspired by a profound belief that you are uniquely created by God and endowed with talents and gifts that are yours and yours alone — and that the discovery and development of these talents is key to your well-being. God wants you to be *you* — not somebody else, but *you*.

The Strengths Movement keeps gathering momentum. More than 3 million individuals worldwide have now taken the Clifton StrengthsFinder assessment, either through one of our several books published for different audiences or through Gallup educational sessions. More than 400 people have gone through Gallup training and become certified Faith Strengths Performance Coaches, specially trained to give individuals one-on-one feedback about maximizing their Signature Themes of talent. And thousands of people have gone through our seven-week small-group program, *The Living Your Strengths Journey*, and begun to find and fulfill a calling based on their Signature Themes.

As you read this book, you'll find that much of the text is the same as that found in earlier editions of *Living Your Strengths*. But you'll also discover a very significant improvement: stories. In preparation for this edition, we asked our strengths coaches to provide examples of transformation — in individual lives and in congregations and parishes as a whole — that strengths development has inspired. As I read these stories, I was inspired and more than a little overwhelmed at the difference a focus on one's greatest talents brought to so many lives.

We've included many of these Strengths Stories at the end of the chapters of this book. For the most part, you're reading the stories just as we received them: Some of them are longer narratives, while others are short vignettes. Some are in first person, and some are in third, as strengths coaches described the impact that talent discovery and strengths development have had on the lives of those they coached. One thing all of the stories have in common: Each one is a powerful testimony to the "strength" of strengths development.

If you've read a previous edition of *Living Your Strengths*, I hope you find this edition to be better than the earlier ones — after all, my Maximizer talents are always driving me to seek constant improvement. And if you're reading *Living Your Strengths* for the first time, you're reading the best version yet! The important thing is that you're on a path of self-discovery that will empower you to be the *you* God created you to be — uniquely designed for strength, so you can live the best version of yourself every day.

Blessings,
Albert L. Winseman, D.Min.
Ideation Futuristic Maximizer Strategic Command
September 2008

FOREWORD

*We are pleased that Bishop William F. Murphy and Monsignor Bill Hanson
each have written a foreword to the Catholic edition of* Living Your Strengths.
We offer our sincere thanks for their contributions.

From Bishop William F. Murphy:

It gives me great pleasure to thank Al Winseman and Curt Liesveld
for preparing and publishing a Catholic edition of *Living Your Strengths.*
Because it is aimed particularly at Catholic parishes and communities, it in-
corporates language and concepts that are familiar to a Catholic audience.

When first I came to know of Gallup's strengths program, I was intrigued by its approach and its goal. The approach of setting a foundation
for growth based upon assessment of one's God-given talents, personal and
communitarian, is a very attractive one, especially in a society that today
seems all too often to stress the negative. The goal of growing in accordance
with our unique natures in order to "be Church" and rejoice in that "being"
seems to me to reflect Saint Paul's call to us all "to live in Christ Jesus."

The Gospel of Jesus Christ is truly "good news." It is the only good
news that never grows stale and that always offers to one and all the promise
of life — God's life given to us by Jesus Christ so that we might live in His
Spirit and give witness of that life to the world. This is the ever-ancient
and ever-new call of Jesus to all his disciples "that the world may believe."
While we rely always on the Word of God that is lived out by us in His
Church through the sacraments, that gift of His grace is offered to us with
a challenge: Can we harness our own gifts and talents as individuals and

as a community to make the "good news" live in our hearts and in our communities?

To my mind, *Living Your Strengths* offers us a combination of human talents and insights that will help any Christian community realize its potential through a renewal of the spirit and a deepening of commitment to live one's faith. I hope that many Catholic parishes and communities will take advantage of this invitation to "become ever more the Church of Jesus Christ" so that the life of Christ might be lived in our parishes more fully and the message of Christ might be more widely believed and praised and proclaimed.

Yours sincerely in Christ,
Most Reverend William F. Murphy
Bishop of Rockville Centre
Rockville Centre, New York
July 2006

From Monsignor Bill Hanson:

A unique code. A mysterious search. A quest for a treasure beyond price.

Does this sound like the makings of a runaway bestseller? All these things are in the book you are holding in your hands: *Living Your Strengths*. In fact, all these things are actually inside of you. They are inside every human being, and they make up the chapters of every hero's journey.

Welcome to the code that will unravel the adventure you have been on since you were born — the adventure of life God gave each of us, and all of us, in the divine image.

Every time you and I ask ourselves, "What should I do next?" or "Why did I react that way?" or "Why do I love doing some things and avoid doing others?" we are trying to decipher the meaning of the mystery of "who I really am." We find ourselves asking these same questions about others in our lives. In this book you will learn the code that will unlock the mystery of yourself, and of every other person you will ever meet.

For almost 35 years as a parish priest, I have had the opportunity to assist my parishioners in cracking the codes within them. I have been privileged to share in hundreds of conversations with individuals trying to understand what God has given them by the Grace into which they have been born and baptized. I have been blessed to hear from some of these same people 20 years later. They tell me how the gifts of God they accepted in themselves led them to risky — but right — decisions, peace of mind, and harmony with others in their family and friends.

I have retold many of these stories in homilies in six different parishes where I have ministered over the years. As a child I was bored in church unless the priest told a good story, so when I became a priest I promised myself I would try to tell the same kind of stories that held my attention growing up. I'm glad that many have found these stories interesting and inspiring. But over all those years, I still felt as if something was missing. It's easy to admire someone else's heroic story and very hard to live your own.

As I've talked with people over the years, I have heard one hope repeated more often than any other by people trying to find their way to God through life: "I wish I could be sure I am on the right track." All the signs, memories, narratives, and other guiding exercises of our spiritual practices help tremendously, yet seem to lack two things: specificity and objectivity. These two missing pieces show up in questions that sound like this: "How can I know what God wants *me* to do?" and "Does anything like this ever happen to anyone else?"

Having collected and catalogued life-changing stories from personal sources, books, movies, and radio, I realize that to adequately answer these questions both specifically and objectively, someone would have to talk to an awful lot of people and then sort through an unimaginable amount of human experience. (I always knew that person would never be me!) To my surprise and delight, I discovered in 2002 that someone had actually done all this work and had made the results available in a simple format.

Dr. Donald O. Clifton of Gallup began this work more than 40 years ago. He recognized that there were patterns in the talents God gave people from birth. He believed that he was called by God to use his talents to help others find theirs. To accomplish this task, he researched the natural patterns of thought, feeling, and action of 2 million people in more than 25 countries. The result is the Clifton StrengthsFinder, an online tool that reveals your top five themes of talent — your Signature Themes. Through this book, you will have access to StrengthsFinder.

Dr. Clifton's work confirms in an objective way that your specific talent patterns are unique to you as an individual. Al Winseman and Curt Liesveld joined Dr. Clifton in this project and have adapted StrengthsFinder specifically for parishes and individual parishioners. They have described the research results for you, illuminated them with stories from parishioners, and identified these talent patterns in passages from Scripture. It is my privilege to write the Foreword for this Catholic edition of *Living Your Strengths*.

Do you know the usual response I used to get from my preaching about the talents God has bestowed on each one of us in our creation in the divine image? "Yes, Father, but I really don't have any talent." By that my parishioners meant they couldn't play the piano or "draw a straight line." And so the Stewardship message about "Time and Talent" missed its mark.

Then we introduced *Living Your Strengths* into the life of our parish. At the time of this writing, more than 200 parishioners have learned their Signature Themes, which hold their greatest God-given talents. We have their pictures and Signature Themes displayed in the lobby of our parish center. We wear our Signature Themes on our parish nametags. One weekend a month, we give away little gifts that are symbolic of the talents from a particular theme. We pray for the development of our talents in a particular theme at the General Intercessions each week.

What's more, the penances I suggest in the Sacrament of Reconciliation are based on a parishioner's God-given talents. My homily stories often name the God-given top themes of the person they describe. Each month a new group of 10 to 14 parishioners forms to meet for four weeks and learn about their own and others' talents more deeply. The members begin as strangers and, in the end, always want to stay in touch with each other.

As our Stewardship of Time and Talent has become so much more specific and objective, the results of gift-based giving have increased dramatically. Attendance is growing, financial and talent gifts are increasing, gratitude and generosity are more evident, and time spent for service in the parish and local community has increased. Large and small projects are easier to carry out because of the heightened spirit of cooperation and mutual respect.

Right after we each learned our individual Signature Themes in my own small church community within the parish, our usual discussions "about" God turned into telling stories of "experiencing" God. We lost track of time and unwittingly acted out something Pope Benedict XVI said in a weekly audience: "We are not the heralds of an idea, but the witnesses of a person." Specifically learning our own God-given talents and objectively seeing the talents of others moved us to a deeper encounter with God in ourselves and in each other.

Our parishioners have three reactions when they take the Clifton StrengthsFinder:

- *Amazement at its accuracy.* "How could they possibly know this about me?" Of course it's based on our own personal responses to the statements in the online survey as well as the patterns of talent that emerge in the context of so many people's patterns of behavior.

- *Genuine surprise.* "I always thought (or was always told) that this particular behavior of mine was a weakness. I never thought of it as a valuable talent!" No wonder Dr. Clifton has been named the Father of Strengths-Based Psychology* for his dedication to focusing on what is right in people.

- *Gratitude.* "In the last three years since learning our Signature Themes, I have come to understand my spouse better than in the previous thirty years." People are also saying this about their teenagers, parents, bosses, coworkers, friends, and even people they consider their enemies!

---

*Donald O. Clifton (1924-2003) was cited in 2002 as the Father of Strengths-Based Psychology in a Presidential Commendation from the American Psychological Association.

Another American psychologist, Carl Rogers, once said, "The most personal is the most general." The deepest things that happen to you are the same things you can be sure are happening to everyone else. That's why I collect life-changing stories from real people. When I retell them in a homily, people recognize the truth in their own experience, in their own souls.

For instance, not long after I had retold the story of how the great seafaring anthropologist Thor Heyerdahl got over his fear of swimming, a mother in my parish told me that, in response to the story, her son had gone to the school library for the first time and taken out a book on Heyerdahl's life. This deep connection between us as God's creations, the uniqueness and the similarity, is what people in our fragmented world are longing to discover. StrengthsFinder is a major contribution to this deeply human yearning.

It is the church's job to lead the way for the world to find this treasure buried in the field of human experience, this pearl of the greatest price. Almost 40 years ago, Joseph Ratzinger described this as the deeply personal and profoundly communal dual nature of faith. The future Pope Benedict XVI pointed to the "Do you believe?"-"I do believe" dialogue formula of the ancient Baptismal Rite as the model for our search for the Kingdom of God. In his *Introduction to Christianity*, he wrote, "In this process of turning about, as which faith must consequently be understood, the I and the We, the I and the You interact in a way that expresses the whole image of humanity…the relationship to God, to the 'You,' and to the 'We' are intertwined…(God) seeks out man in no other way but in his fellow humanity."

My parishioners act out of this truth when they ask not only, "Am I on the right track?" but also, "Is this happening to everyone else?" The Clifton StrengthsFinder is the most practical empirical tool I have ever seen assist parishes in the compelling task of unifying human life. Pope John Paul II wrote about a "spirituality of communion" in his encyclical *At the Start of the New Millennium*: "Brothers and sisters in the faith should so regard each other as 'those who are part of me.'" One of my parishioners told me she was a lot nicer to the other women at work because she learned her Signature Themes. When I asked her why, she said, "Well I realize now more than ever that I have my way of doing things based on my talents, and they have different talents and other ways of doings things. So my way isn't the only way."

There you have it: deeper self-respect, deeper mutual respect. And God is easier to find in just such a world. It is a more grateful, graceful world. It is a more Eucharistic world, proclaiming the mystery of faith in all the ways we use our gifts.

I am deeply grateful to Gallup for sharing their research with us and helping us become a more grateful parish. My personal life is richer, and our parish life is more abundant for the blessings that the authors' God-given talents, shared so generously, have brought to us.

A man in my parish makes the following petition during the General Intercessions at Mass every day: "May we have the grace to discover God's will for us and the courage to carry it out." This book is the answer to that prayer. It will bless you by uncovering your own unique code, on your mysterious search, for the treasure beyond price, which God has already given to you.

Monsignor Bill Hanson, Pastor
Church of St. Gerard Majella
Port Jefferson Station, New York
The Feast of Pentecost
June 2006

INTRODUCTION

American churches are experiencing a power shortage. It's not the kind of problem that can be fixed by opening natural gas fields or drilling oil wells or building electrical plants. The shortage is in fulfilled human potential. In churches all across the United States, people aren't harnessing the power of their innate gifts. They are not fulfilling God's purpose in their lives. And most people don't even know it.

A recent national study by Gallup uncovered the roots of this problem. It revealed that most people (53%) do not strongly agree with the statement "In my parish, I regularly have the opportunity to do what I do best." Clearly, too many individuals' talents and strengths are going unrecognized and unappreciated. And this adds up to an enormous loss of human potential that could be tapped for the transformation of society.

We need a revolution in our parishes — a strengths revolution. This book was written to get that revolution started.

THE FOLLY OF "WEAKNESS PREVENTION"

If you're like most people, you have grown up with the "weakness prevention" model. You've been told that to become strong, successful, or truly serve God and the world, you must "fix" your weaknesses. You've been told that your talents and strengths are a source of sinful pride. What you really need to do, the "weakness experts" say, is to develop your areas of *non-talent*. Then, they believe, you will be ready to fully serve God and the world.

That thinking is just plain wrong.

In Gallup's research into human potential over the past 30 years — including interviews with more than 2 million people — the evidence is overwhelming: You will be most successful in whatever you do by building your life around your greatest natural abilities rather than your weaknesses. *Your talents should be your primary focus!* The problem is that most people don't even know what their greatest talents are or how to go about discovering them. *Living Your Strengths* will help you do that.

As you read this book, remember that God has given you a unique combination of talents. God also places within you a calling — a calling to serve others and advance the cause of Christ and the Church, a calling to ministry. Your calling is what God wants you to do with your life; your talents and strengths determine how you will get it done. When you discover your talents, you begin to discover your calling.

Like everyone, you've been blessed by God with a deep reservoir of untapped potential. That potential is your talent, waiting to be discovered and put to use in your life. It's time for you to unleash the power of that potential and begin to discover your unique talents.

Start by taking Gallup's Clifton StrengthsFinder, an online talent assessment. You'll find instructions on how to take the Clifton StrengthsFinder on the following page. Then get ready to embark on an adventure sure to change your life.

Take the Clifton StrengthsFinder®

We recommend that — before you continue reading — you take the Clifton StrengthsFinder 1.0 assessment at sf1.strengthsfinder.com. You will need the unique access code from the insert in the back of this book.

CHAPTER 1

The Power of the Right Fit

To understand how parishes often fail to tap the natural abilities of their parishioners, consider the story of Liz and Rick.

A married couple in their early thirties, Liz and Rick moved to a new city, and after getting settled in their new home, started attending Mass at the parish in their neighborhood. They had been active in their former parish and wanted to get involved in their new parish. They weren't quite sure what they wanted to do, but they knew they wanted to do a lot more than just attend Mass. So one evening, as they were reading the weekly parish bulletin, they decided to send the parish ministry coordinator an e-mail introducing themselves and saying they wanted to get involved.

They soon got a call from the parish ministry coordinator asking them if they would be greeters for Mass during July. Rick and Liz agreed and dutifully showed up to shake hands with parishioners for five Sundays in July.

The couple had almost diametrically opposed reactions to the experience. "I loved it!" recalls Liz. "This was great. I like meeting new people, and being a greeter made me feel like I was making a contribution to my parish. I'd do it every week if I could!"

But Rick's reaction was not so positive. He remembers, "It was like pulling teeth. I was really uncomfortable. I didn't know what to say or what to do. It doesn't come naturally for me like it does for Liz. I guess I'm just shy by nature. I sure hope no one asks me to do this again."

By asking Rick and Liz to serve as greeters, the parish ministry coordinator was subscribing to the myth that "an active member is a faithful member." The coordinator must have thought, "Anybody can be a greeter. After all, it's a great way to get to know the members of the parish." So she asked Liz and Rick to fill roles in the parish without first discovering their natural abilities — their talents. She lucked out with Liz, who will likely become more engaged by the experience. But if she continues to ask Rick to be a greeter, he will become disengaged very quickly.

Why did Liz and Rick react differently? Because Liz loves to meet new people and to win them over. In her world, there are no strangers, just new friends she hasn't met. So being a greeter fits naturally with Liz's innate abilities. Rick, in contrast, doesn't want to meet and greet a stream of people. It makes him uncomfortable and doesn't come naturally to him. Rick would rather deepen existing relationships than form a bunch of new ones.

Rick's predicament is all too familiar in parishes across the country. How about you? Have you found your "place" in your parish? Do you have the opportunity in your parish to do what you do best on a regular basis — to use your talents and strengths? Do you find joy, satisfaction, and growth in the ways that you serve God, your parish, and other people?

If you answered "no" to any or all of these questions, read on! Your parish life — not to mention your personal, family, or professional life — could be a lot more fulfilling. The first step is defining what a strength is — and what it is not.

WHAT IS A STRENGTH?

To begin to know and live your strengths, you need to understand what a strength is. A **strength** is the ability to provide consistent, near-perfect performance in a given activity. This ability is a powerful, productive combination of talent, skill, and knowledge.

To better understand what a strength looks like, consider Steve, who for the past 20 years has been teaching Church history classes at his parish. His classes are always among the most popular offered, and he often draws a standing-room-only crowd. "I got started doing this by volunteering to help Father Warren, our pastor, teach a six-week class on the Gospel of Mark during Lent one year," he recalls. "I teach training classes at work, and I thought I'd give it a shot. I loved it! Even though that first class went well, I knew I wanted to get a lot better at it."

Over the years, Steve has audited classes at the Jesuit university in his community, taught himself elementary Greek, subscribed to a Church history magazine, and learned to do multimedia presentations to enhance his lessons. "I'm a much better teacher than I was twenty years ago. It's definitely been worth the effort." Steve started out with some natural talents for teaching, and by adding skills and knowledge to that naturally powerful foundation, he built a strength.

The key to building a strength is first to identify your dominant themes of talent, then delve into those themes to discover your greatest talents, and finally produce a strength by complementing those talents with knowledge and skill related to the task.

Talents are naturally recurring patterns of thought, feeling, or behavior that can be productively applied. Unlike skills and knowledge, talents naturally exist within you and cannot be acquired. They are your inborn predispositions. They are the things that you do instinctively and that naturally give you satisfaction. Your spontaneous, top-of-mind reactions to the situations you encounter are the best indicators of your talents. Everyone is talented, but we recognize some people's talents more easily than others — simply because these people are in roles that they consistently perform with excellence and because the roles are suited to their natural predispositions.

What does a talent look like? A talent can be the natural tendency to:

- be competitive

- pick up on the emotions of others

- thrive under pressure

- make others laugh

- enjoy puzzles

- recognize the uniqueness in others

- envision and clearly articulate a future scenario

Skills are basic abilities to move through the fundamental steps of a task. They can be acquired through formal or informal training. Once you've acquired the skills necessary for a given activity, you have the ability to perform its steps at base-level ability.

What does a skill look like? A skill can be the ability to perform the fundamental steps of:

- adding and subtracting

- processing a customer's insurance claim

- using software to prepare a presentation

- giving a patient an injection

- preparing a lesson plan

- checking someone into a hotel

Knowledge is, simply, what you know. You can acquire knowledge through education or training. It may be factual knowledge, like the words of a foreign language, the books of the Bible, software features, or the table of periodic elements. It also may be experiential knowledge, which isn't taught in classrooms or in manuals. Experiential knowledge includes the insights or awareness you have gained through experience.

What does knowledge look like? Your knowledge could tell you:

- how to deal with an upset customer

- how to cope with job-related stress

- what time Mass is held at your parish

- the FAA's safety regulations

- what part of a lesson your students find most difficult

- the fastest route to the grocery store

- why and how Martin Luther started the Protestant Reformation

An important difference between talents and skills and knowledge is that although skills and knowledge can be acquired, their applicability is restricted because they can be very situation-specific. Just because an individual is a successful accountant doesn't mean that person could also be a successful heart surgeon. The skills and knowledge needed for accounting are very different from those needed for heart surgery. However, given enough time, commitment, and opportunity to learn, an accountant could learn the skills necessary to be a heart surgeon, and vice versa. But talents are a different story. Without possessing the talents for those activities, the heart surgeon could not *excel* as an accountant, and the accountant could not *excel* as a heart surgeon.

Talents are transferable from situation to situation. The hotel desk clerk who instinctively knows just the right way to make a guest feel welcome and at home would most likely be an excellent greeter for worship services at his or her church. Skills and knowledge can be acquired, but they will not significantly help you unless they enhance a talent.

The apostle Paul is a perfect example of someone whose talents remain constant in different situations. Before his conversion on the road to Damascus (Acts 9), Paul — who was then known as Saul — was stubborn, single-minded, and zealous in his attacks on Christians. After his conversion, Paul was stubborn, single-minded, and zealous in his defense of Christianity. His conversion did not change his talents. What changed for Paul as a result of his conversion were his *values*. After his encounter with the risen Christ, instead of using his talents to hunt and persecute Christians in an effort to destroy the Church, Paul was using those same talents to seek and convert non-Christians with the intent of growing the Church. The same talents that made him such a formidable enemy of the Church were now making him its invaluable champion.

The fundamental building block of any strength is talent. When you enhance a talent by adding the right skills and useful knowledge, you have created a strength. Again, to live your strengths, you must first identify your greatest talents. By taking the Clifton StrengthsFinder, you identified your top five themes of talent — your "Signature Themes."

A THEOLOGY OF STRENGTHS

There is something about the concept of talents and strengths that just "feels right." When we discover our talents, when we give them a name, something resonates deep within us. It is as if our spirits react to this discovery with a resounding "Yes! This is the way it is supposed to be — this is who I was created to be." And we find it somehow freeing; naming our greatest talents sets us free to develop them and live through them. Naming our top talents gives us permission to accept our areas of lesser talent and either discard them or manage them. It gives us permission to stop trying to be who we are not and concentrate on who we are — who we were originally created to be.

The Judeo-Christian tradition affirms what we already know in our souls. Consider these passages from the Old and New Testaments:

- The first creation story in Genesis, the first book of the Old Testament, depicts a scene of beauty, serenity, and goodness. The crowning achievement of Creation was humankind:

God created man in his image;
in the divine image he created him;
male and female he created them.

God looked at everything he had made, and he found it very good...
Genesis 1:27, 1:31

- In the book of Jeremiah in the Old Testament, we find this:

The word of the LORD came to me thus:
Before I formed you in the womb I knew you,
before you were born I dedicated you,
a prophet to the nations I appointed you.
Jeremiah 1:4-5

- In his first letter to the Corinthians, the apostle Paul points out that members of the Church each have different gifts and talents, which are to be used for the good of the entire Church:

There are different kinds of spiritual gifts but the same Spirit; there are different forms of service but the same Lord; there are different workings but the same God who produces all of them in everyone. To each individual the manifestation of the Spirit is given for some benefit.
1 Corinthians 12:4-7

From a spiritual viewpoint, when we deny our talents and instead focus on our weaknesses, on some level, we are telling God that we know best and that God somehow made a mistake in gracing us with our unique mix of talents.

Consider the Hasidic tale of the Rabbi Zusya. When he was an old man, Zusya said, "In the coming world, they will not ask me: 'Why were you not Moses?' They will ask me: 'Why were you not Zusya?'"** That is God's question to each of us as well. We are not expected to be who we are *not*. We are expected to be who we *are*.

We hope that this book will help you discover and affirm your areas of greatest talent and help you learn ways to live through your God-given talents in your parish, as well as in your personal and professional life. At the very least, we hope that when you finish this book, your active involvement in your parish won't be frustrating like Rick's, but as fulfilling and inspiring as Liz's. Only by knowing your talents and strengths and by living through them can you be the best *you* that you can be.

**Martin Buber, *Tales of the Hasidim: The Early Masters* (New York: Schocken Books, 1975), p. 251.

STRENGTHS STORIES

Counseling About Competition

Dan and Renee, a couple engaged to be married, came to me for premarital counseling after I had already met with each separately for strengths performance coaching. I was honored that they asked. Soon after the session began, they described his Futuristic talents and her Context talents. We discussed the ways in which their talents in these two very different themes complemented each other and sometimes caused conflict.

Dan and Renee were elated by these conversations. Even Dan, who by nature is usually very quiet, talked eagerly about how the session was helping him gain insights about his future wife as well as himself.

But the best part of our meeting was when Renee talked about how Dan's Competition talents drove her nuts. She felt she disappeared completely from his life when sports were on the TV or they were at a game. She confessed to feeling threatened by his competitive nature, and she feared that during sporting events they would lose their close connection.

In response, I asked them if there was a way they could use Dan's Competition talents as the foundation for strength in their marriage rather than a threat to Renee. At first they had no answer, but they thought about it together until they began to share stories about how much fun they have when they go for walks. Renee said, "Sometimes we will see a telephone pole and we'll race each other to see who can get there first." "Yeah," Dan said. "And we sometimes play the smallest and most meaningless games together, but we have a blast!"

I repeated the question: "So, again, in what ways could you two use competition to strengthen your marriage instead of threaten it?" And over the next 20 minutes, they came up with a bunch of great ways to connect with each other over his competitive nature. I think they laughed together that whole time as they created really fun ways for them to play and compete together, even if he didn't win all the time. At the end of the session, Renee told me she was grateful for learning how appealing to Dan's Competition talents could be a really great way to connect with him.

Marc Otto
San Diego, California, United States

The Communicator

Since my earliest memories, I have been in love with words; I've always been a communicator. The media have changed at times, but enthusiastic fascination with communication has always been a cornerstone of my personality. However, it wasn't until I learned about the talents represented by the Communication theme that I really started to understand why and how I was drawn — even driven — to communicate.

Before discovering my Communication talents, I wondered, for instance, why sometimes I would quibble with one word in a sentence of forty, or one sentence in the midst of a thousand. And why would I insist that using one synonym over another could change the entire meaning of a sentence? Or that moving a sentence from the beginning of a paper to the end could change the direction of the entire argument? Why would I argue about "semantics" in even the most insignificant discussions?

When I read the Communication theme description, I realized that this drive toward perfect communication is a talent — and not a weakness. I'd been accused of being picky, elitist, or a perfectionist my entire life for behaviors that I was now being taught were actually opportunities for strength. It was like being set free, not just *from* something, but *toward* something. Not only was I released from false expectations; I also felt challenged to fulfill the potential of these raw talents. And the beauty of this development process is that no matter how many strengths I create by building upon my Communication talents, the raw, yet powerful potential never diminishes.

Strengths development is the lifelong maximization of an infinite resource. Every beautiful sculpture, once finished, leaves in its wake another new block of marble, every bit as perfect and inviting as the one before it.

Rebecca Syme
Bozeman, Montana, United States

Boosting Her Confidence

Knowing my Signature Themes explained many of my most common behaviors and has boosted my self-confidence by validating my decisions and actions. For example, Responsibility is one of my top themes. I rarely take the easy route, but now I know why — and I appreciate my Responsibility talents instead of berating myself for them.

Knowing my Signature Themes also has made it okay for me to be an achiever. In corporate America, women sometimes suffer harsh criticism for being ambitious, but having Achiever among my top themes gives people a much more positive view of my need to get things done and move on to the next goal.

Putting a name to my talents also positively affects *my own* perception of my value. I knew I like to read and try new stuff, but I didn't know I was a Learner. I didn't know I was Futuristic; I thought I just had an active imagination.

Knowing my Signature Themes gives me the confidence to put my talents into action and thoroughly apply them in my life. And conversely, also knowing the themes in which I'm not as talented, I'm aware of when to call for help and how to pick complementary team members. I wish I had known my Signature Themes 25 years ago — it would have saved me much second guessing.

Dea Wilkins
Lutz, Florida, United States

Building on His Own — and Others' — Talents

Barrie is a very experienced manager of motor vehicle service operations, be it car, van, and truck service or accident repair. He has consistently increased profits for the companies where he has worked. In his latest role as a service manager in a large van-and-truck service operation, Barrie was able to triple profits in less than three calendar years. As I began to coach Barrie about his talents, I asked him how he managed to achieve that profit increase. His answer was that he is a positive person who sets a target and achieves it, but he could not more specifically identify the attributes that made him so uniquely capable of producing remarkable increases in profit.

I encouraged Barrie to learn about his five Signature Themes, which are: Arranger, Futuristic, Ideation, Positivity, and Individualization. As he read the descriptions of those themes and we talked through what he had done to increase profits, Barrie was really pleased to be able to identify that…

- When he first took on the role, he surveyed the service area and visualized what the department would be like if it were working at its best. He envisioned a tidy and professional work environment in which the staff would become motivated and feel valued and in which productivity and profitability would increase as a result. He now has an understanding of his Futuristic talents and how he used them as the starting point every time he took on a new service-management role. For Barrie, the starting point is always this: Visualize the future.

- He recognized that to increase profits, he would have to spend more than his initial budget allocation and would need to get his own manager to approve a spending increase. He also had to persuade staff who said, "We have never done it that way" to accept and even embrace change. Barrie's positivity about the results he could produce helped him get the full backing of the General Manager and the staff to make changes. He now understands how his Positivity talents contribute to his success.

- During his first week, he arranged "one-on-one" meetings with each and every member of the team in random sequence, irrespective of the individuals' titles in the organization. *Everyone* was to feel important and valued. He gained an understanding of each individual's current work role, the specific activities that he or she did best (their strengths), and his or her aspirations for the future. Just as importantly, he wanted to learn about each person's interests and family background. All seemed very willing to share. Equipped with that information, Barrie adapted each person's role to get the best from that individual. His approach increased motivation and made the staff feel valued. He now understands how his Individualization talents have contributed to his success.

- Barrie asked the individuals for insights about how the department could work better, and he held specific Profit Clinics to which staff members were invited. He used these forums to encourage creative thinking about how the department could improve. Implementing their good ideas added to the motivation. He also had ideas of his own and asked the staff to assess their soundness. He now understands how his Ideation talents have contributed to his success.

- Barrie deliberately assigned to his unit leaders both authority and responsibility to bring about the needed changes, and he avoided interfering in their roles. Although that arrangement took away some of Barrie's ability to directly implement change, and in a sense intensified the stress on him, it increased the unit leaders' ownership of the actions and outcomes, and it created a true team effort that ultimately produced the desired considerable change. He now understands how his Arranger talents have contributed to his success.

Barrie has learned the secret behind this strength — his ability to consistently create a highly profitable service department — is recognizing and building upon his greatest talents and those of everyone in the department. He now looks at new challenges and plans to tackle them by specific use of talents from each of his top themes. And with the language provided by those themes, he can explain the strengths development concept to anyone.

Frank Bennett
Exeter, Devon, England, United Kingdom

CHAPTER 2

Finding the Right Fit

At an early age, you started hearing it: It's a virtue to be "well-rounded." You were told that this was your ticket to teachers' approval, straight A's, a great college, a successful career — not to mention money, happiness, and fulfillment. Through schooling, training, and societal expectations, you got the message: Soften your sharp edges. Become smooth and well-rounded. (They might as well have said: Become as dull as you possibly can be.)

Here's the problem: Conventional wisdom doesn't consider who you really are. And besides, *God didn't make you well-rounded!*

Why don't you start, right now, to defy that "wisdom" — and begin appreciating your unique, God-given talents? Individuals become strong by recognizing and using those unique talents as the foundation for developing strengths.

When we focus on our talents, we are more effective at our tasks and roles. We are also more successful, happy, and fulfilled. Just ask Father Dan. Reflecting on his years as a pastor, Father Dan realized that even though public speaking didn't come naturally to him, he nevertheless was an effective preacher because he focused on his talents. "The times I seemed to get the most positive feedback on my homilies were the times I was able to link a concept with a personal story — when I was able to be the most authentic or transparent as a person," he says.

Father Dan was able to do this because of his talents in Relator, one of his Signature Themes. "Relators want to be real; they want to be authentic; they want to be themselves," Father Dan says. "I was pretty comfortable doing that, even in front of a bunch of people. Now, these were obviously people that I knew pretty well, and so I was willing to let them know who I was. I think it helped me be a better communicator sometimes. Even though I wasn't a natural communicator in front of people, I think it was my Relator and maybe my Learner talents that helped me to do that. I like to learn stuff and then make it real through my own stories."

Just as Father Dan's greatest talents did for him, your dominant natural responses will determine how you approach a challenge, relate to others, and fulfill God's purpose for your life.

By now, you should have taken the Clifton StrengthsFinder assessment and learned your Signature Themes. (If you haven't taken the assessment, take it now before you read on.) Your Signature Themes are the key to helping you find the right fit, for they are the key to discovering the ways in which you most naturally think, feel, and behave as a unique individual. They very likely reveal things you "can't not do." To help you get more familiar with your Signature Themes, we suggest you do the following:

- After completing the assessment, print your Clifton StrengthsFinder Signature Themes report. Carefully read and re-read the descriptions of your Signature Themes. Knowing that each description is essentially a set of examples of talents found in that theme, consider the talents it presents. Which of these talents do you feel are most prevalent in you? Which are less prevalent? Can you think of other talents in this theme that might be dominant in you? Don't limit yourself to the talents in the description.

- So you can become more and more familiar with your talents, try to read through the descriptions at least once a day for three weeks — about the length of time some behavioral scientists say it takes for an activity to become a habit. Consider how well each of the talent examples "fits" you. Then, go through the theme descriptions with a highlighter in hand. Highlight the portions that best represent you. Remember that a theme is simply a category of talents, and that even though you have many talents in each theme, some of those talents are more natural to you than others. Highlighting the talents that best describe you will help you better understand how your talents in that theme operate in your life.

- Because our own talents are such a natural part of us, we are often blind to them and their value. To truly see our talents and their valuable influence in all our decisions and actions, we need another person to "hold up a mirror" for us. To see your talents "reflected in the mirror," tell two people (individually) about your Signature Themes — family members, coworkers, friends, or anyone else with whom you would enjoy having this discussion. Describe your top themes to them, and then ask them to tell you about times when they have seen these themes at work in your life.

As you become more aware of your own greatest talents and how you live through them, you will begin to discover the "right fit" in all areas of your life: your relationships, your work, your volunteering, and your spirituality. Chapters 4 and 5 will help you explore this in greater detail.

HELPING OTHERS FIND THE RIGHT FIT

Whether you are a pastor, parish staff member, or lay leader, surely you collaborate with other people to accomplish the mission of your parish. Understanding your talents and strengths, and those of the people you work with, can dramatically improve your effectiveness and accomplishments.

When you understand the strengths approach and put it into practice, you realize that capitalizing on what you and those around you naturally do best is so much more productive than trying to "fix" yourselves.

It took Bonnie a couple of tries before she found a role in her parish that was right for her. She was fairly new to her parish and wanted to get involved. So one Sunday, she answered a plea from the religious education director to be a youth group sponsor. "I thought, 'How hard can that be?' I was young (or so I thought). I had been a teenager once, so I thought I could relate to them," she remembers.

Bonnie was wrong. "It was a disaster," she says. "The lessons were frustrating. I couldn't relate to the kids. Their questions always caught me off guard and I felt stupid. Fortunately — for me and the kids — I was able to get out of it, and they found a much better sponsor." Bonnie then tried ushering and discovered she wasn't very good at that either. She didn't have a knack for thinking on her feet or for meeting new people.

One day, Bonnie noticed that the parish grounds needed "sprucing up" with some flowerbeds. She says, "I summoned my courage and went to the property committee and asked if I could do that — and to my surprise they said, 'Go for it!' So I got to plan the flower arrangements — the types and colors, the location, all of that. I'm really into detail and order, and I seem to have a knack for putting together patterns of colors. And I just love to garden. It was a perfect fit, and I couldn't be happier."

It's a good thing Bonnie was persistent. Others might have just given up after experiencing only one disappointing "wrong fit."

MANAGING LESSER TALENTS

Truly successful and fulfilled people like Bonnie know the deep truth of this maxim: *You will be successful because of who you are, not because of who you are not.* How can you help people do what they naturally do best rather than try to "fix" them? How can you position people in your parish so that they can develop strengths while furthering the mission of your parish? You'll find the answers in the following four proven management tactics.

Whenever possible, avoid using your areas of lesser talent. A lesser talent becomes a weakness *only when you try to use it.*

Lisa grew up in a small town and attended a very traditional parish. "Sometimes I felt a lot of pressure to do things that were just very foreign to me," she says. In the small-town parish, there was an unspoken expectation that women were the ones who were supposed to volunteer to work in the nursery. "After all, it's taking care of kids, and women are supposed to be more nurturing, right? Well, that just wasn't me," Lisa remembers. "But now, at this parish, there's no pressure to be something you're not, and so I decided to get involved in the music ministry. I discovered that I love to sing, and I'm not half bad, even though I've never sung in public before. It's refreshing not to feel like I have to do something I'm not good at."

Use support systems. The majority of adults in this country have one shortcoming in common, and we use a support system to manage this imperfection. The weakness is our eyesight. Every morning, millions of us wake up and immediately use a support system — our glasses or contact lenses — without giving it a second thought. If you are a pastor, when you get up to preach every Sunday, you most likely use a support system: a microphone to help your voice project so you can be heard.

There's a story about a prominent Protestant minister who was getting ready to lead the congregation in The Lord's Prayer. He stood up in the pulpit, faced his congregation of several hundred people, and began by saying, "Let us join together in the prayer our Lord taught us." He continued, "Now I lay me down to sleep, I pray the Lord my soul to keep." When he noticed that no one was praying, the pastor realized what he was saying and stopped in mid-sentence. He looked at his congregation for a second, and then, without a word, stepped down from the pulpit and walked off through the door at the side of the chancel into his nearby study.

The pastor sat down at his typewriter, opened his Bible to Christ's Sermon on the Mount, and tapped out the words to The Lord's Prayer. When he finished, he went right back into the pulpit and tacked the freshly typed words to the prayer right in the middle of the pulpit, where he would be sure to always see it.

As if nothing had happened, he started over, "Let us join together in the prayer our Lord taught us." And never again did he rely on memory when leading the congregation in The Lord's Prayer — he had a support system.

Establish complementary partnerships. When God spoke to Moses through the burning bush and called him to go back to Egypt to lead the Israelites to freedom, Moses was full of excuses about why he wasn't qualified. Moses told God, "…I have never been eloquent, neither in the past, nor recently, nor now that you have spoken to your servant; but I am slow of speech and tongue" (Exodus 4:10). So God found Moses a partner — Moses' brother Aaron. Moses had the talent for leading and for devising strategy, but he couldn't wow a crowd with his oratory or stand before kings and summon the appropriate words. Aaron could. And together, Moses and Aaron made a great team — which got even stronger with the addition of their sister Miriam. Power struggles notwithstanding (see Numbers 12), this trio brought their individual talents and strengths together into a combination — a complementary partnership — that multiplied their effectiveness exponentially.

Examples of effective team building can be found in everyday life too. Jay, the president of the parish council, learned the same lessons that Moses did. "Chairing our parish's strategic mapping team was one of the most rewarding experiences of my spiritual life," says Jay. His parish was at a crossroads, and the pastor put together a team that was charged with rewriting the parish's mission, vision, and values statement. The team members would also restructure the parish's organizational plan to reflect the new statement, and they would propose major program changes to better carry out the parish's mission.

"It was daunting," Jay recalls. "I still think the pastor had some divine intervention in choosing the team, because the combination of talents represented by the nine of us was perfect for the task." Some of those themes still stick out in Jay's mind. "I have Focus, Arranger, and Command in my Signature Themes, so I was able to keep us on track, juggle our responsibilities, and keep us moving toward action — as well as make some tough decisions when disagreements occurred."

Two members of Jay's team, Adam and John, had Futuristic and Strategic among their top themes, so they were able to paint the picture of what their church could be like 10 or 15 years down the road — and then sort out the options for getting there. Another team member, Amy, had exceptional Analytical talents, and she kept everyone asking the right questions. "She really made us do our homework to make sure we were on the right path," Jay says.

Of two other team members, Jay recalls, "Terry had great Belief talents that were so valuable in helping us assess our values, and Sonya's Positivity kept things fun — which was such a blessing when we were doing such important work. Our teamwork was a great success, and now — seven years later — our parish is still relying on the work we did."

There is no denying the power of the right fit when building teams. The right combination of complementary talents produces powerful results.

Leverage your own talents and strengths. Another way to manage your weaknesses is to rely on your strengths to overcome your lesser talents. "I even surprised myself when I volunteered to work as a counselor in our crisis center," says Robert. "I mean, I'm not a 'touchy-feely, tell-me-all-your-problems' kind of guy. People tell me I can be pretty insensitive, and I guess that's true — a lot of times I'll hurt someone's feelings without even realizing it."

At first glance, the counseling role didn't seem like it would be a good match, but something inside kept urging Robert to do it. "I think it was God telling me to stretch myself," he says. "Anyway, I've always been interested in psychology, what makes people tick and stuff, and I really wanted to help."

So Robert jumped in and found out that he really enjoyed it — and his supervisor has given him a lot of positive feedback. "I'm able to listen to people's problems without getting emotionally involved and then help them sort out options in a nonjudgmental way," he says. "Of course, I'm smart enough to know when I'm in over my head and when to refer someone to a professional. But for a rank amateur, I think I do all right!"

Robert doesn't have much talent in Empathy, so he doesn't instinctively draw on that theme to help those who talk to him. But his talents in the Restorative and Strategic themes make up for this and enable him to be involved in a ministry he really is passionate about.

TALENTS, STRENGTHS, AND SPIRITUAL GIFTS

You may be wondering how discovering your talents and building and applying strengths fits in with the concept of Spiritual Gifts. Paul makes several references to Spiritual Gifts in his letters in the New Testament, and no two references are exactly alike:

Then since the gifts that we have differ according to the grace that was given to each of us: if it is a gift of prophecy, we should prophesy as much as our faith tells us; if it is a gift of practical service, let us devote ourselves to serving; if it is teaching, to teaching; if it is encouraging, to encouraging. When you give, you should give generously from the heart; if you are put in charge, you must be conscientious; if you do works of mercy, let it be because you enjoy doing them.
Romans 12:6-8 (NJB)

There are many different gifts, but it is always the same Spirit; there are many different ways of serving, but it is always the same Lord. There are many different forms of activity, but in everybody it is the same God who is at work in them all. The particular manifestation of the Spirit granted to each one is to be used for the general good. To one is given from the Spirit the gift of utterance expressing wisdom; to another the gift of utterance expressing knowledge, in accordance with the same Spirit; to another, faith, from the same Spirit; and to another, the gifts of healing, through this one Spirit; to another, the working of miracles; to another, prophecy; to another, the power of distinguishing spirits; to one, the gift of different tongues and to another, the interpretation of tongues. But at work in all these is one and the same Spirit, distributing them at will to each individual.
1 Corinthians 12:4-11 (NJB)

And to some, his "gift" was that they should be apostles; to some prophets; to some, evangelists; to some, pastors and teachers; to knit God's holy people

together for the work of service to build up the Body of Christ, until we all reach unity in faith and knowledge of the Son of God and form the perfect Man, fully mature with the fullness of Christ himself.
Ephesians 4:11-13 (NJB)

We don't want to get into a discussion about the Spiritual Gifts of healing, miracle working, or speaking in tongues. That's not our area of expertise, and theologians and biblical scholars have debated the meaning of those Gifts for centuries. But if you look at the other Spiritual Gifts that Paul lists — teaching, evangelization, leadership, and such — you will see that these Gifts really describe functions of ministry within the Church.

These Spiritual Gifts, then, perhaps more accurately can be called ministry areas, or areas of calling. Paul does, however, make it clear that these Gifts are to be used for the betterment and advancement of the Church: "to equip the saints [members] for the work of ministry, for building up the body of Christ."

Through the centuries, Christians have sought to identify and put into practice their unique Spiritual Gifts or callings. Identifying your talents isn't intended to take the place of identifying your Spiritual Gifts, but rather, it can be a powerful way to enhance your Gifts and calling. Your Spiritual Gifts help you find *what* the ministry is that God wants to see you accomplish; your talents are God's way of showing you *how* you will accomplish it.

Ron and Gina understand this. Along with being members of the same parish, they have much in common: Both believe they have the Spiritual Gift of evangelization; they both have a passion for sharing their faith so that others may discover the abundant life they have found as followers of Jesus Christ. However, their talents are somewhat different. Ron's Signature Themes include Communication, Woo, and Significance, while Gina's include Relator, Empathy, and Harmony.

"My involvement in prison ministry has been life changing, not to mention eye opening," says Ron. "I lead a Bible study there once a week, and it's a real challenge. A lot of times guys will show up just to do something — anything but sit around their cell. And they'll come in with this chip on their shoulder, like, 'You aren't going to reach me with this Jesus stuff.' And I make it my personal mission to reach guys like this, and I see their lives begin to change when they open up to God's love. It's such a rush for me to see them start to respond and know that I was the one God used to reach them." Ron's success in his Spiritual Gift of evangelization depends on his productive application of his natural talents.

So too with Gina, whose "heart just aches when I see my friends going through rough times." She says, "Those are the times when I feel God can use me to either revive or deepen someone's faith." Gina wants all her friends to know how much they can depend on God to see them through the tough times of their lives — that all they have to do is turn to God, and God will be there. "Their lives would be so much more satisfying," she says, "and things would go so much smoother for them if they turn all their problems — their entire lives — over to God for His direction." So if Gina knows someone well enough, she'll talk to them about what a difference her faith has meant to her. "It's really just being a friend, that's all," she concludes.

Both Ron and Gina are living out their Spiritual Gifts of evangelization. But the ways they do it — the steps they take to achieve their outcomes — are totally different. They are different because Ron and Gina have different talents.

If you have started the process of helping people in your parish discover their Spiritual Gifts, then helping them do the same with their talents would provide a powerful combination. Identifying Spiritual Gifts defines the outcome; discovering talents defines the steps.

STRENGTHS STORIES

A Tough Decision

Four years ago, I was a high school assistant principal entering the thirtieth year of my career. My strong record as an assistant principal and building administrator led to my being offered the choice of three new positions: middle school principal, high school principal, or assistant superintendent for curriculum and instruction. I eliminated the middle school choice immediately because the vast majority of my career was spent in the high school setting. However, I was torn between the two remaining choices: principal of a newly constructed high school (403,000 square feet in size, 2,600 students, 360 faculty and staff) or assistant superintendent in a school district that enrolls more than 15,000 students, contains 12 elementary schools, 4 middle schools, and 2 high schools.

Although I enjoyed working with faculty, staff, and students in the school setting, I was thinking, "Isn't it the aspiration of all school administrators to move into a district administrative capacity? To work at the district office?" Further compounding the issue, I was flattered by the district office offer because the traditional pathway to that opportunity includes tenure as a school principal — yet here I was, possibly going straight from an assistant principal to assistant superintendent.

I spent three difficult days trying to decide my future. My wife and I talked about virtually nothing other than this decision during those three days. I would wake up each day with one choice in mind, think about it during the day, and go to sleep changing my mind, only to think about it during the night and change my mind again by morning. I sought the counsel of some of my closest friends; they all felt I should take the district office position because I could best serve the district in that role, but even with that advice, I remained conflicted and unable to come to a decision to which I could fully commit.

I decided to look at my options from a different perspective: Rather than try to fit myself to one of the two positions, I decided to fit the positions to me. I had worked with my small church community as a facilitator to help the members identify and understand their Signature Themes. My own top five themes are Relator, Context, Includer, Arranger, and Harmony.

Looking through the lens of my Signature Themes, I quickly came to realize that my choice was very easy to make: I would find personal fulfillment and best use my greatest talents if I were able to work with groups of individuals to achieve common goals and encourage others to be a part of that common vision. I also thrive on handling multiple challenges (my wife often tells me I never finish one thing before moving on to the next) and enjoy the challenge of helping to mediate and resolve differences of opinion. The opportunity to use my talents in those ways was simply much greater in the high school setting than at the district office level.

The fog of indecision immediately lifted, and I could clearly see that the high school principal role would be the best fit for *me*. I put aside flattery and ego and informed the superintendent of my choice.

He wanted me to take the district office position, and he tried to convince me to do so, but I held my ground and explained the basis of my decision to him, and he respected my reasoning. I have now been the high school principal for three years and have not regretted my decision for one minute. Quite honestly, had I not looked at this decision through my Signature Themes, I probably would have taken the district office position — and I would not be as professionally and personally fulfilled as I am today.

John Aleksak
Port Jefferson Station, New York, United States

A Girl's Inspiring Discovery

At Mosaic, our church in Los Angeles, we hold an event that includes Clifton StrengthsFinder assessments. After the most recent event, I announced that I would create a new focus group to provide more thorough guidance and coaching. Ten people joined the focus group, and I spent several hours coaching each individual in a small group, with the hope that each of them learns from others.

One of the girls said, "I have often wondered if I have talents. And even if I do have talents, I've questioned whether I have the ability to use them to help others. Our group coaching not only revealed that I have valuable talents; it also gave me the profound realization that I can use my talents to leverage the talents of others. There's a compounding effect of living a strengths-focused life, and I can't wait to do this more."

Steve Saccone
Los Angeles, California, United States

Battling Her "Basement Behaviors"

When Cathy first discovered her Signature Themes, she immediately connected with Achiever and Responsibility. She recognized that those themes had long paired to make her successful as a mother and a volunteer. Nonetheless, it was in that pairing that she also often saw her biggest weaknesses. As much as she appreciated her reliability, consistency, and productivity, she was equally frustrated with her tendencies to over-commit and take responsibility for other people.

That frustration soon lessened. As Cathy learned more about her Achiever and Responsibility talents, she began to recognize her "basement behaviors" and started whittling them away. She knew she would often say, "I know this is my Responsibility talking, but ..." and then rationalize a behavior she didn't want to commit. As she processed these behaviors (through her Input, Ideation, and Learner talents), she was able to sort the truly productive behaviors from those that were destructive.

The most amazing part of Cathy's transformation is that she now recognizes her "basement behaviors" before she commits them, and then chooses a wiser course. In essence, by better understanding her Responsibility and Achiever muscles, and by consciously complementing them with talents from her other top themes, she has become able to apply them even more powerfully.

Cathy also has become more aware that the ways in which she applies her talents can affect others. She recently went through a move with her aging mother and was the one sibling who took responsibility for helping her mother clean out the house they had grown up in. She noticed, as she was doing this, her refined use of her Responsibility talents. Cathy calls this a shift from "taking care" to "giving care." She feels that "taking care" is the controlling, raw Responsibility thing to do. It's a way of making her feel strong at the expense of someone else. But "giving care" is respectful of the other person — like asking her mother what she wants to throw away instead of making decisions for her. Giving care strengthens both parties, not just one. Giving care is a dialogue, not a monologue, and it maximizes the value of Responsibility talents.

Rebecca Syme
Bozeman, Montana, United States

CHAPTER 3

Creating Strengths-Based Parishes

What would the Church (or an individual parish, for that matter) look like if leaders and members embraced a strengths-based approach to ministry? What if every Christian was encouraged to actively develop and use his or her talents to strengthen the Body of Christ and further the mission of the Church universal? Just imagine!

But before we take off into the realm of those possibilities (a real treat for those of you with Ideation or Futuristic among your Signature Themes), let's first explore how the early witnesses to the faith described the Church. We'll see that those witnesses focused on individuals' talents and the development of strengths when organizing this fledgling community. Indeed, their approach two millennia ago — spelled out explicitly in the New Testament — is as relevant as ever today; the Church urgently needs a strengths-based revitalization.

Let's be honest: The modern Church — not just Catholic, but Protestant and Orthodox too — is in trouble; most people don't find its message relevant. But it wasn't always that way. In the beginning, the Church was bold and transformational. People's lives were changed by the message of salvation and by belonging to a community in which dramatic change was the norm. Finding salvation in Jesus Christ encouraged people — set them free, really — to focus on being the unique individuals God created them to be. And by living in community with others who had discovered this truth, they found opportunities to "build each other up" — to encourage one another to discover their talents, build strengths, and maximize their gifts.

Early leaders of the Church truly believed that Jesus' life, death, and resurrection had ushered in a "new Creation," or at least the realization of God's original intent of Creation. They believed that they were living at the beginning of the time when God was "making the whole of creation new" (Revelation 21:5) (NJB). This created a sense of excitement, of urgency, in everything they did. They invited friends, neighbors, family members, and even strangers to "come and see" the new thing that God was doing in their midst. They wanted others to experience the new life they had found in Jesus and to know the fulfillment they had found living out this new life with others who had experienced it.

There was, to be sure, a missionary zeal among the leaders of the early Church. Luke's account of the birth of the Church — in the New Testament's Acts of the Apostles — is replete with stories of the early leaders' missionary journeys. Peter and the rest of the disciples, and Paul and his partners Barnabas, Silas, Timothy, and others, all traveled outside the bounds of Judea to spread the Gospel (the story of Jesus' life, death, and resurrection) and what it meant to have "new life in Christ." Early believers were encouraged to find their place in the new community and to discover their gifts in order to be truly fulfilled as followers of Jesus.

To better understand how the early Church transformed not only individual lives, but also the social fabric of first-century Palestine, let's dig deeper into three key New Testament passages. Within these passages — Acts 2:43-47, Acts 6:1-7, and 1 Corinthians 12:12-27 — are clues to building a strengths-based parish and Church.

The evangelist Luke was a key witness to the power of the early Church, and he wrote about this power in his Gospel and in Acts; together, the Gospel of Luke and the Acts of the Apostles make up one-quarter of the New Testament. In the second chapter of Acts, Luke gives us an important insight into the essence of the early Church:

> *Awe came upon everyone, and many wonders and signs were done through the apostles. All who believed were together and had all things in common; they would sell their property and possessions and divide them among all according to each one's need. Every day they devoted themselves to meeting together in the temple area and to breaking bread in their homes. They ate their meals with exultation and sincerity of heart, praising God and enjoying favor with all the people. And every day the Lord added to their number those who were being saved.*
> Acts 2:43-47

In these five verses, Luke describes what it meant to live in response to the good news of Jesus' life, death, and resurrection: Unity in spirit and in life, care for the poor, and the worship and praise of God. Let's look at these points a bit more closely.

The early Church lived out unity in spirit and in life. Even the casual reader of this passage from Acts will notice that the unity Luke stressed was a hallmark of the early Church; its members "had all things in common." The Church broke down the social barriers that were entrenched in the first-century Roman Empire. Unlike life in Roman society, in the Church, the poor interacted with the rich, the uneducated with the educated, the men with the women — and all were considered equal.

What mattered was not wealth or social position or gender, but a belief in Jesus Christ and the talents, strengths, and gifts that individuals could bring to and develop in the new community. In the early Church, people were valued for who God created them to be, not for the role they were forced to conform to in Roman society.

The early Church cared for the poor. In this instance and others, Luke described a community in which the needs of the poor were addressed. In some instances, the members of the community shared their possessions with the poor. In other instances, individual members kept their possessions but gave liberally of what they had so that the poor were supported.

The important thing to note is that, in a rigidly stratified society in which wealth and poverty were seen as divine reward and punishment, the Church went against the cultural norm and said that individuals matter. Because individuals were uniquely created by God and reconciled to God through Jesus Christ, the members of the Church had a responsibility to ensure that everyone's basic needs were met. After all, how were individuals going to develop strengths, make the most of their gifts, and fulfill God's purposes for their lives when they were in need of such basics as food, clothing, and shelter?

The early Church praised God. The leaders of the early Church never forgot that God was the source of all they were and all they had. They were not "self-made" by any means; most of the original leaders were Jesus' disciples, and most of them were peasants. They were ordinary people with no designs on greatness.

But they realized that they were called by God to proclaim the good news of God's love for humanity — a love poured out in the life, death, and resurrection of Jesus Christ. Each of them had talents, and God used those unique talents to start a movement — through these ordinary people — that would change the world. The early Church kept its focus on the source of strength and new life and hope, never passing up an opportunity to praise and worship God.

THE EXPONENTIAL POWER OF DELEGATION

Due to the enthusiasm and authenticity of this diverse group of believers, the Church grew quickly. The appeal of the message, the promise of new life, and the acceptance and celebration of individual uniqueness formed a powerful combination that made this new movement an irresistible force. But the rapid growth created a problem: The original leaders, the apostles, couldn't do everything themselves. They needed help.

Indeed, the apostles were confronted with a valid complaint: Some of the widows were not getting their daily allotment of food. This was a critical concern because in first-century culture, widows were among the most vulnerable members of society. In a time when a single woman earned little, if anything, widows were dependent on the kindness of others. The early Church made a commitment to care for the "least of these," just as Jesus had taught them. As a result, the leaders felt it was their obligation as followers of Christ to ensure that the poor and the destitute were cared for. And, the vast majority of widows fell into this category. So when the apostles learned that some of the widows weren't being fed, it was cause for alarm.

But they were in a bind. The apostles were the primary leaders of the new movement, and most of their time and energy was spent casting the vision, preaching and teaching, and seeing to the spiritual growth and health of the community. What's more, their talents, gifts, and callings were to leadership. Looking after the widows required *management*.

At first, the apostles tried to lead *and* manage — which is how they found themselves in this predicament in the first place. The solution they devised was elegant in its simplicity and brilliant in its clarity: Why not find others who have the talents, gifts, and calling for administration?

> *About this time, when the number of disciples was increasing, the Hellenists made a complaint against the Hebrews: in the daily distribution their own widows were being overlooked. So the Twelve called a full meeting of the disciples and addressed them, "It would not be right for us to neglect the word of God so as to give out food; you, brothers, must select from among yourselves seven men of good reputation, filled with the Spirit and with wisdom, to whom we can hand over this duty. We ourselves will continue to devote ourselves to prayer and to the service of the word." The whole assembly approved of this proposal and elected Stephen, a man full of faith and of the Holy Spirit, together with Philip, Prochorus, Nicanor, Timon, Parmenas, and Nicolaus of Antioch, a convert to Judaism. They presented these to the apostles, and after prayer they laid their hands on them.*
>
> *The word of the Lord continued to spread: the number of disciples in Jerusalem was greatly increased, and a large group of priests made their submission to the faith.*
> Acts 6:1-7 (NJB)

Clearly, when people serve in roles that fit their talents and gifts, God does marvelous things.

PAUL'S WISDOM AND MINISTRY

The book of Acts isn't the only place in the New Testament where we find clues about how strongly the leaders of the early Church felt about the uniqueness of individuals — a uniqueness created by, blessed by, and encouraged by God. In Acts, Luke tells us about one of the greatest leaders of the early church: the apostle Paul. We also have Paul's own words in the New Testament. As a leader of the Church, Paul wrote letters of instruction to churches he founded — and several of those letters are contained in the New Testament.

Paul was born "Saul" in the ancient Near Eastern city of Tarsus (in what is present-day Turkey), a Jew by birth who was also a Roman citizen. As an adult, he became a Pharisee, a recognized expert on Jewish religious law. By Luke's account and by Paul's own admission, Paul persecuted the members of the early Church. And according to Luke in Acts 7-8, Paul (Saul) was present at the stoning of the first Christian martyr, Stephen.

Acts 9 recounts Paul's dramatic conversion to Christianity on the road to Damascus, where he encountered the risen Christ and was confronted with his persecution of the Church. After his conversion, Paul traveled throughout the Mediterranean, founding several churches in the major cities of the area. And when he finally reached Rome, he died as a martyr to the faith he once set out to destroy.

Paul's letters offer a fascinating and important glimpse into the inner life of the early Church. They also provide insight into the most powerful theological mind of the first century. For our purposes, we've chosen to focus on a profound idea that Paul shared with the Church at Corinth. In the twelfth chapter of his first letter to the Corinthians, Paul explains how each member of the Church is part of the Body of Christ, and just as the different members of the physical body have different functions, so too do the members of the spiritual Body of Christ:

For as with the human body which is a unity although it has many parts —
all the parts of the body, though many, still making up one single body — so
it is with Christ. We were baptised into one body in a single Spirit, Jews as

well as Greeks, slaves as well as free men, and we were all given the same Spirit to drink. And indeed the body consists not of one member but of many. If the foot were to say, "I am not a hand and so I do not belong to the body," it does not belong to the body any the less for that. Or if the ear were to say, "I am not an eye, and so I do not belong to the body," that would not stop its belonging to the body. If the whole body were just an eye, how would there be any hearing? If the whole body were hearing, how would there be any smelling?

As it is, God has put all the separate parts into the body as he chose. If they were all the same part, how could it be a body? As it is, the parts are many but the body is one. The eye cannot say to the hand, "I have no need of you," and nor can the head say to the feet, "I have no need of you."

What is more, it is precisely the parts of the body that seem to be the weakest which are the indispensable ones. It is the parts of the body which we consider least dignified that we surround with the greatest dignity; and our less presentable parts are given greater presentability which our presentable parts do not need. God has composed the body so that greater dignity is given to the parts which were without it, and so that there may not be disagreements inside the body but each part may be equally concerned for all the others. If one part is hurt, all the parts share its pain. And if one part is honoured, all the parts share its joy.

Now Christ's body is yourselves, each of you with a part to play in the whole.
1 Corinthians 12:12-27 (NJB)

If the Church was to be true to the purpose for which God intended it, Paul asserted, then individual talents and gifts needed to be not only recognized, but celebrated. If we look more closely at these verses, we'll see that Paul is essentially advocating a strengths-based parish.

Unity in Christ. This letter to the Corinthians, like all the other letters in the New Testament, was not written in a vacuum. Paul was addressing some specific problems that had arisen in the young Corinthian Church.

There were some in the Church at Corinth who believed that some talents and Spiritual Gifts were more valuable than others, and that members who had these "special gifts" were more important than other members of the Church.

Paul wrote to correct that misguided notion, and he began by reminding the Corinthians that all gifts come from the Holy Spirit and that all members of the Church are one in Jesus Christ. Neither birthright ("Jews or Greeks") nor social position ("slaves or free") makes any difference; we "were all baptized into one body" and "made to drink of one Spirit." If a parish is truly to become strengths-based, it must never forget that its foundation rests upon unity with all other Christians in Jesus Christ.

Diversity of talents and gifts. After establishing that the foundation of the Church is unity in Christ, Paul launched into his brilliant comparison of the metaphorical "Body of Christ" to an actual human body. Just as the human body is made up of many parts, so too is the Body of Christ. The entire human body isn't an ear or a hand or a foot or an eye, but rather is made up of many parts, each with different functions.

Paul said it is like that in the Church — the Body of Christ — as well; the Church isn't made up entirely of prophets or teachers or counselors or administrators. There is a diversity of talent in the Church just as there is a diversity of functions of the parts of the human body. And members of the Body of Christ shouldn't all strive to have the same talent or gift, just as ears shouldn't strive to be eyes or hands strive to be feet.

The whole is greater than the sum of its parts. The human body is a marvel to behold. When it is functioning properly, the ears hear, the eyes see, the feet walk, the heart pumps blood — all the parts work together in harmony. But when one part of your body isn't working properly, perhaps due to injury or illness, it affects everything else. If you've ever experienced the truth of the adage "When your feet hurt, you hurt all over," you can better understand Paul's words: "If one part is hurt, all the parts share its pain. And if one part is honoured, all the parts share its joy" (NJB).

Paul's illustration points to an important truth: *We need each other.* Together, as the Body of Christ, we can accomplish so much more than we ever could alone. When we recognize, celebrate, and develop the diversity of talents that live among us, we are fulfilling God's purpose not just for our individual lives, but also for the Church.

THE STRENGTHS-BASED PARISH IN THE 21ST CENTURY

The idea of the strengths-based parish, with its roots in the early Church, is not relegated solely to the first century. There are living, breathing examples of strengths-based parishes flourishing today. Stories about people whose lives have changed have been pouring out from these parishes. We'd like to share some of these stories.

Father Bill, a pastor in a mid-sized parish in New York, discovered the amazing power of focusing on strengths when his study group decided to get together after a summer break. The group hadn't jelled, and Father Bill was looking for a way to help the members really become a "group," not just individuals who occasionally get together. Father Bill suggested that they share a Clifton StrengthsFinder experience. "Everyone was up for it," Father Bill says, "including some who hadn't been showing up at all."

Eleven group members participated, with one member acting as the facilitator. "In the first week," Father Bill reports, "everyone got their books, and the facilitator led us through some activities that helped us gain a better perspective on the whole idea of discovering talents and building strengths. By the second week, we all went online to take the Clifton StrengthsFinder, and each one, to a person, found it to be uncannily accurate. Good discussion followed."

Father Bill says, "But the third session broke the bank at Monte Carlo! We formed groups that were designated by our Signature Themes, and we shared how we've helped people by using our talents and strengths. As we did this, there was a growing openness and ease among the group members, almost like time-lapse photography. You could actually see and feel a level of freedom and engagement taking place right before your eyes. It was noticeably more relaxed and more intense than anything we had experienced in three years of meeting."

They formally ended the session and gathered for some refreshments. Father Bill says, "No joke, the conversation that spontaneously followed was mind-blowing! Each person was speaking about his or her faith experiences to a degree that was at once relaxed and unbelievable. One man even turned to his wife and said, 'I don't think I ever told you this dear, but...' One story of spiritual experience and commitment led to another, and all of a sudden, it was 20 minutes to midnight, and no one noticed the time passing."

There was no doubt in the group members' minds that going through the strengths exercises for three weeks inspired them to share their faith in a way that they hadn't in three years. "In fact," Father Bill says, "it was fascinating to hear people comment on the stories by pointing out each other's talents and strengths in action. Amazing! Everyone had heartfelt expressions of gratitude for being able to share their deepest faith experiences with others who didn't think they were nuts, but quite genuine."

Father Bill continues, "These are the tools to get the Church back on track, to turn over the soil, to get rid of the thorns and weeds, and to be able to produce a hundredfold from the seed God has already sown. Discovering our talents has definitely been a tipping point!"

In fact, discovering talents and building strengths has implications beyond your parish. Knowing and living your greatest talents is a powerful way to positively influence others' lives. Consider the story of one of Father Bill's parishioners, Mike, who is a member of the parish council and actively involved in various other ministries. Last year, the small Bible study group Mike belonged to decided to focus on discovering their talents, and each member took the Clifton StrengthsFinder assessment. Mike learned that among his five Signature Themes were Maximizer, Arranger, and Relator — themes of talent that he could readily see at work in his life.

Mike had worked for 15 years at the local Honda dealership, starting right out of high school and working his way up to become the manager of the parts department. His department was arranged for maximum efficiency. When his mechanics needed a part, he always knew where the part was, and he never let his inventory run low on any part. He had invested time and energy in maximizing his mechanics' productivity, and he took pride in seeing to it that they had everything they needed to be successful in their jobs. His top themes made him successful and appreciated at the Honda dealership — until it was sold.

The new owners weren't concerned about relationships with customers or employees — relationships that had made the dealership successful over the years. Consequently, many long-time employees left for other jobs. One day, a former employee, who had landed a job at a larger Honda dealership in a different part of the city, called Mike to tell him about an opening for a parts department manager. Mike decided to apply for the position, and in the interview, the owner asked Mike what he thought his strengths were. Mike replied, "I not only think I know what my strengths are, I actually know my top five themes of talent." Mike described each of his Signature Themes and how they help him succeed in work and life.

"Where did you learn this?" asked the astonished owner.

"In my small church group," replied Mike.

"No kidding?" remarked the owner. "You mean you actually learned something useful at church?" Mike got the job, and the owner started attending Mike's church.

One day, Father Bill stopped by the dealership to see how Mike's new job was going. "Like the Maximizer and Arranger he is, Mike had the parts department organized and humming along at maximum efficiency," Father Bill says. "But the really remarkable thing was the look on the mechanics' faces when they came to Mike with parts needs and questions." They were happy, relaxed, and seemed to truly enjoy Mike's presence. Father Bill asked one of the mechanics about it, and he said, "Before Mike came, all the mechanics were ready to quit. They were so frustrated by the disorganization in the parts department and the shabby way the parts manager treated them." But when Mike came on board, there was a huge change in attitude and performance — and the mechanics stayed. Mike was able to bring out the best in them because he was living through his greatest talents and the strengths he had built upon them.

As Mike's story illustrates, we take our talents and strengths with us wherever we go, and the positive effects benefit not only ourselves and our fellow parishioners, but also our family, our friends, and our coworkers. Discovering talent and building strengths is also a way for those who are already engaged in their parish to find a better fit for themselves. Janice's story is a case in point.

Janice was always active in her large Midwestern parish. In fact, her pastor says that she is one of those people who can sometimes get too busy. Among other things, Janice had created her parish's women's faith enrichment program from scratch. She developed the topics, found the curriculum, coordinated teachers, and in general, created a growing spiritual formation program that is the "crown jewel" of the women's ministry in her parish. But after accomplishing all this, she was starting to feel somewhat empty — even a bit restless.

When her pastor offered a class on strengths, Janice signed up and discovered her five Signature Themes. As she learned about her talents, she realized why she was feeling restless. Achiever and Maximizer are two of her top themes, so maintaining a ministry at its current level — even if that level is excellence — isn't going to fulfill her. As an Achiever, she needs to feel like she's accomplishing something, moving forward. And her Maximizer talents drive that momentum toward excellence. She realized that she felt like she had accomplished all she could with the women's ministry, and maintaining the program at its current level was not going to be satisfying. She needed a new challenge. She needed something she could work hard at developing and taking to excellence.

After several discussions with her pastor and the leader of the women's ministry, Janice is now developing a parish-wide program to focus on talent discovery and strengths development (which plays right into her Maximizer theme). It's a lot of hard work, but Janice once again feels personally fulfilled and spiritually nourished — because she is in a ministry that helps her maximize her talents.

EVERYONE NEEDS A COACH

One of the keys to Janice's success was that she had a "coach" — someone in her parish who talked to her one-on-one about her talents. Janice's coach gave her valuable feedback on her talents and showed her how her talents are at work in her life (and come as naturally as breathing). Because of this, Janice began to see ministry opportunities in which she could be successful because of those talents.

If we accept the fact that our Signature Themes are the primary lenses through which we see the world, then we also must accept that we are in many ways blind to our own talents. We need others to help us see our talents and strengths and help us develop them to their full potential. As Proverbs 27:17 (NJB) states, "Iron is sharpened by iron, one person is sharpened by contact with another." A trusted advisor who acts as a coach can help "sharpen our edges" and help us fulfill our potential.

Rhonda's experience with a coach changed both her marriage and her ministry. Because she was new to her parish, taking the Clifton StrengthsFinder was a quick way to plant her feet firmly within the parish. After just a one-hour "coaching session," Rhonda was able to walk away with a new understanding and perspective on her marriage (both she and her husband, Dave, had taken the Clifton StrengthsFinder). By learning their Signature Themes, Rhonda and Dave learned more about each other and why they acted and thought the way they did. The Clifton StrengthsFinder opened up a whole new path of communication for them and gave them a new language to describe why and how they act the way they do.

Rhonda also discovered a ministry area in her parish that fit her talents. With exceptional talent in themes like Discipline, Relator, Communication, Activator, and Command (and the Spiritual Gifts of Exhorting and Encouraging), along with a passion for writing, Rhonda quickly agreed to be a part of the creative writing ministry at the parish. Her first writing assignment was to encourage the rest of the parish by sharing her own story of how God had affected her marriage and family.

A good coach can help people see talents and strengths that they often cannot see for themselves. Chris, who has had a great deal of experience coaching others in her church, was helping her friend Angie discover how to best apply talents from her Signature Themes to her life and work.

Chris says that Angie was able to see how her talents applied to her work at the office. However, understanding how she was using them in her family life was not as clear. One morning, they were sitting in Angie's kitchen discussing her talents. In the middle of their conversation, the phone rang. A family member had just died, and funeral arrangements were in progress. "From the sound of things," says Chris, "some family members were upset and unsure how best to handle everything. But Angie knew just the right things to say and do. I started jotting down notes about the conversation, and when Angie hung up the phone, I handed her my notes — notes that related the phone conversation I overheard to her Signature Themes: Harmony, Arranger, Empathy, Context, and Restorative."

As Angie looked at Chris' notes, she started to see the relationship. "I began to connect the dots," says Angie. "I understood how my areas of talent guided my interaction with my family members." Angie's talents helped calm the waters of a crisis.

TALENTS: MAKE THE MOST OF THEM

Before we close this chapter, we want to examine one more New Testament text — a text that is perhaps more relevant than any other concerning talents, strengths, and gifts and the importance of using them wisely. According to the Gospel of Matthew, the following is one of the last parables Jesus told his disciples before his passion, death, and resurrection:

> [Jesus said]: *"It is like a man about to go abroad who summoned his servants and entrusted his property to them. To one he gave five talents, to another two, to a third one, each in proportion to his ability. Then he set out on his journey. The man who had received the five talents promptly went and traded with them and made five more. The man who had received*

two made two more in the same way. But the man who had received one went off and dug a hole in the ground and hid his master's money. Now a long time afterwards, the master of those servants came back and went through his accounts with them. The man who had received the five talents came forward bringing five more. 'Sir,' he said, 'you entrusted me with five talents; here are five more that I have made.' His master said to him, 'Well done, good and trustworthy servant; you have shown you are trustworthy in small things; I will trust you with greater; come and join in your master's happiness.' Next the man with the two talents came forward. 'Sir,' he said, 'you entrusted me with two talents; here are two more that I have made.' His master said to him, 'Well done, good and trustworthy servant; you have shown you are trustworthy in small things; I will trust you with greater; come and join in your master's happiness.' Last came forward the man who had the single talent. 'Sir,' said he, 'I had heard you were a hard man, reaping where you had not sown and gathering where you had not scattered; so I was afraid, and I went off and hid your talent in the ground. Here it is; it was yours, you have it back.' But his master answered him, 'You wicked and lazy servant! So you knew that I reap where I have not sown and gather where I have not scattered? Well then, you should have deposited my money with the bankers, and on my return I would have got my money back with interest. So now, take the talent from him and give it to the man who has the ten talents. For to everyone who has will be given more, and he will have more than enough; but anyone who has not, will be deprived even of what he has.'"
Matthew 25:14-29 (NJB)

We find it significant, of course, that the word for the amount of money Jesus was talking about in the parable — talent — is the same word we use for "a pattern of thought, feeling, or behavior that can be productively applied." The point of Jesus' parable, which some people understandably see as harsh, wasn't about investing huge sums of money (the amount of money given to the slave who received five talents would be worth about one million dollars today!), but rather it was about using the talents that God places within each one of us. God expects us to develop those talents and use them wisely.

Notice that not every slave was given the same amount of "talents"; each was given, said Jesus, "according to his ability." So it is with God and the distribution of talents and gifts among individuals. Our coauthor, Don Clifton, was always fond of saying that each person can do something better than 10,000 other people. The key is for individuals to discover what that something is, and then do it.

In this parable, Jesus is expressing the same idea about God. The master gave each slave a sum of money that he expected the slaves to invest on his behalf while he was away. Then, upon his return, the master asked for an account of what each slave did with the money. The slaves who received five talents and two talents doubled their investment, and the master was pleased. The slave who received one talent did nothing with his, and the master was far from pleased; in fact, he was furious. Notice that the "one-talent" slave didn't lose the money. He kept it safe, thinking that his master would be pleased to just get back what was his. But the master had the opposite reaction; he wanted the slave to take a risk and grow his talent.

Indeed, developing our talents into strengths requires risk. We must step out, try new things, or take a chance by doing something we may fail at — at first. But if we do not take some risks — emotionally, physically, and spiritually — we will never grow.

God expects no less from us and from the Church.

STRENGTHS STORIES

Eliminating the Negative

Discovering our strengths as a team has completely changed the way we conduct our ministry. Every relationship is more significant, every individual is more unique, and every communication is more complete. My job as a team leader has become easier as each member of the team has discovered not only his or her own greatest talents, but also the talents of his or her coworkers.

In our church we have a fairly large staff, and each staff member has his or her own idea of what things should look like, how ministry should be accomplished, and what the final product should look like. Through individual discovery, team blends, and continual assessment of top themes within the team, we have found ways to work together more solidly, and we have eliminated much of the negative connection between staff members. Our focus is now solely on the team's ministry, rather than on roadblocks.

Julie Giles
Lutz, Florida, United States

Building Trust and Open Communication

After almost four years of serving on the leadership team, I had yet to fully know or understand those with whom I was working. The extent of our personal knowledge about one another went little beyond being asked to "share your favorite movie." At the initiation of new team leaders, we underwent strengths coaching, both individual and team. Everyone engaged in the process, and I learned more about my teammates in one evening than in all my previous years on the board. It was the most meaningful and significant time we've spent together.

Since that time, I have gained a new confidence in my peers. I know their strengths. I know who to look to when faced with a difficult problem and who will resolve a conflict. I know who needs a lot of information to make a decision and who needs very little. And I know my own role in relationship to those of everyone else.

This knowledge builds trust, opens communication, and promotes efficiency. For a board that makes significant long-range decisions, that's crucial. It's the best thing we ever could have done as a team.

Heidi Zwart
Lino Lakes/White Bear Lake/Spring Lake Park
Minnesota, United States

From Pest to Productive Pinch-Hitter

Mary is a retired transportation executive in her early 60s who offered to help with many ministry programs. But her running assessment of just about every program (coupled with advice on how she could fix things if she intervened) had earned her a reputation as a pest.

However, Mary's and our growing understanding of her Signature Themes — Adaptability, Maximizer, Connectedness, Developer, and Strategic — helped her find a more productive role as "pinch-hitter" who steps in on short notice as an emergency substitute for a number of programs. Her Adaptability talents help her respond to these urgent challenges, while her Maximizer talents help ensure a quality job. Program coordinators now turn to her in last-minute situations as a welcome source of strength rather than an annoyance.

Steve Hallmark
United States

Grandma Finds New Callings

Susan's five Signature Themes are Empathy, Connectedness, Developer, Harmony, and Belief. She has been a quiet, faithful, behind-the-scenes member of our church for many years. Immediately after learning her top themes, she articulated great doubt that her talents suited her for any ministry. She just couldn't sense any direction from God in the process of discovering her greatest talents. But, as we further discussed the ways in which she used her talents with her family, several insights came to light.

Susan is the matriarch of her family. Her children and grandchildren consistently turn to her empathizing heart when they're in trouble. They lean on her Belief and Connectedness talents when circumstances make them question why things are happening to them. She is always able to give them insight and encouragement; she's truly the glue that holds her family together. I asked her if she didn't think — that if the only calling she ever fulfilled was to be the best "Grandma" in the lives of her grandchildren — she wouldn't consider herself a great success? She immediately brightened and said, *"Yes!"*

Nevertheless, in the following weeks, Susan used that initial realization to consider other areas to which God might be calling her. In our last small-group meeting, Susan offered input on one of the conversation questions, and I (trying to be affirming) responded by saying, "Sounds like the World's Greatest Grandma to me!" She said, "Now you've got me pegged as just a grandma, but I'm telling you I have strengths that other people haven't even seen me use yet!" Now she's looking at the possibility of helping us network people of differing strengths together to meet needs and problem-solve throughout the church.

Kevin Hopkins
Choctaw, Oklahoma, United States

Instant Bonding

Last year we formed a new Pastoral Council, consisting of nine members plus myself. At the first meeting, everyone, of course, wore nametags so they could learn one another's names. I also asked everyone to go through a StrengthsFinder assessment before our second meeting, which would take place a month later.

At the second meeting, we did about an hour's worth of exercises related to strengths. As I was collecting the nametags at the end of that meeting, I casually asked if people needed to use them for our next (third) meeting. I was greeted with a spontaneous roar of, "Not after what we just did with one another!" It was the fastest bonding I've seen in a group in 35 years of experience.

Vincent Rush
West Babylon, New York, United States

A Feeling of Freedom

About a year and a half ago, our staff spent a day with a coach who shared with our team an all-new concept. This fresh approach contradicted what most of us had been trying to do: Focus on our flaws and the flaws of those around us while spending time trying to repair them and us. Simply stated, the talent discovery our team went through that day has had lasting implications in the way we approach our work as well as in the ways we relate to one another.

Here in the youth staff, we have learned to embrace and value one another in terms of our greatest talents. As a result, we intentionally validate one another. This has enabled us to function with greater unity and at a higher capacity. The strengths language has become a part of our daily vocabulary. The atmosphere created by a focus on talents and strengths development is exciting and productive.

Personally, as I spent time discovering my talents, the Developer theme was my favorite. The freedom I began to experience in developing teams, systems, programs, middle-school students, and volunteers has impacted multiple layers of my life.

It is such a joy to function in the freedom of my strengths! My life has become much more productive and satisfying. I am actually living life in the way God wired me to do it. As a mother, I have even taken time to lead our family through the process of discovering their greatest talents recently on a family vacation. We had some exciting conversations on that road trip, and our family experienced a time of celebrating one another.

Our youth office now relies on the Clifton StrengthsFinder. Summer interns, new team members, core youth leaders, and volunteers are joining the excitement as we discover our talents and learn to function on the premise that we become strong in the areas of our greatest talents in order to honor God in all we do.

Sherrie Leatherwood
Lutz, Florida, United States

An Astounding Transformation

Miracles are happening. The transformation has been swift and profound. Amelia, a staff member responsible for a major ministry initiative, was somewhat removed and gave a vague project update with little information. When asked to make decisions, she was unable. Paul, the team leader, was disappointed.

Two weeks later, Amelia took the StrengthsFinder assessment and had an initial coaching session. Later, at a routine meeting, Paul asked her what she thought the impact of the ministry would be. Amelia quickly answered — using her Strategic talents. She explained exactly what she wanted to happen and thoroughly outlined a full strategy filled with specific detail that would make it happen. Paul was astounded and later asked what caused such a marked change. Amelia replied that it was learning her Signature Themes and as a result, giving herself permission to do what God wired her for.

Kristy McAdams
Lutz, Florida, United States

A More Creative Team

Our entire staff learned our Signature Themes and then participated in coaching. The experience began to change how we looked at one another. If we needed Focus talents, we knew to whom we could turn. Our Ideation person could spin out ideas, and we could then find a person with great Responsibility talents to follow through.

Each new member of the team now receives a StrengthsFinder assessment and strengths performance coaching. The coaching helped us see where our strengths were and what kind of support we could be to one another. It has been an interesting and liberating experience that has caused us to grow personally and to become a more creative and resourceful team.

Nancy Nelson Elsenheimer
Phoenix, Arizona, United States

CHAPTER 4

The World of Talent: Your "Best You" in 34 Themes

As human beings, we all have a special relationship with God that makes us unique when compared to the rest of creation. The Biblical witness affirms this over and over again: In Genesis, we find that "God created man in his image; in the divine image he created him; male and female he created them" (Genesis 1:27). In Psalm 8, the psalmist writes, "When I see your heavens, the work of your fingers, the moon and stars that you set in place — What are humans that you are mindful of them, mere mortals that you care for them?" (Psalm 8:4-5). And Luke's gospel records Jesus as saying, "Are not five sparrows sold for two small coins? Yet not one of them has escaped the notice of God. Even the hairs of your head have all been counted. Do not be afraid. You are worth more than many sparrows" (Luke 12:6-7).

Furthermore, your Signature Themes — your "top five" themes of talent — are unique to you. In fact, your chances of meeting someone with the same Signature Themes, regardless of order, are *less than 1 in 275,000*.

And as incredible as it may seem, there is only a *1 in 33 million* chance that you will meet someone whose Signature Themes match yours and are in the same order. Now *that's* unique!

You've had an opportunity to begin to get familiar with your Signature Themes of talent in your Clifton StrengthsFinder report, read about how the lives of others have been transformed by the application of their greatest talents, and start imagining your life and your church focused on building strength rather than fixing weakness. Now we need to gain some clarity about what your Signature Themes are and are *not*.

A theme is a category of talents, and your Signature Themes are the five categories in which your talents are greatest, as indicated by your responses to StrengthsFinder. A theme of talent is not a strength, in and of itself, even if it is one of your Signature Themes. Your Signature Themes are simply a starting point for discovering your greatest talents, and a strength — the ability to consistently deliver near-perfect performance in a specific task — is what you create when you add helpful knowledge and skills to your talents.

Let's say that Command is one of your Signature Themes. That doesn't make it a strength, but it does mean that your Command talents are some of the ways in which you most naturally think, feel, and behave as a unique individual. Your Command talents could serve as the foundation of a strength, such as the ability to be an advocate for the downtrodden. And to create that strength, you acquire skills and knowledge that will combine with your talents to give you the ability to consistently perform that task at a nearly perfect level.

Obviously, if you want to perform at the level of strength, you must apply your talents, skills, and knowledge in a productive way. Individuals with Command as a top theme tend to take charge, feel a need to share their opinions, and be direct or even blunt in their communications with others. So without complementary talents from other themes, and without the appropriate skills and knowledge, a person with exceptional Command talents might be perceived as bossy, domineering, and rude. But with those important assets, he or she could also perform with strength — say as a voice for the powerless.

Talents do not exist in a vacuum; your talents modify, influence, and enhance each other. Because of the interdependence of your talents, no two Signature Themes will look exactly the same in two different people.

Take the case of Rashon and Michael. They are on the same leadership team in their parish, and both have Ideation as their top Signature Theme — so their planning meetings are never lacking new ideas. But the way their Ideation themes play out is quite different. Rashon also has Communication as another of his Signature Themes, so he has to "think out loud" and verbally process his new ideas when they occur to him. Michael, however, has Intellection among his Signature Themes, so he has to "think it through" whenever he has a new idea — and mentally rehearse the way he will talk about his new idea before he says anything about it. Both have Ideation, but because of their other top themes, they express it differently.

The pages that follow feature descriptions of each of the 34 themes of talent, along with Scripture passages and insights intended to help you recognize and affirm your talents in these themes. We encourage you not only to focus on your Signature Themes, but also to read about the other 29 themes. Your talents are not limited to your Signature Themes. You have supporting themes as well, and reading through the other themes and finding places where these themes resonate with you can give you clues to your talents in those themes. We hope that as you dive more deeply into the world of talent, you will recognize and appreciate that your talents are not only a gift from God, they are also the foundation on which you can excel and lead a fulfilling life through strengths.

ACHIEVER

Your Achiever theme helps explain your drive. Achiever describes a constant need for achievement. You feel as if every day starts at zero. By the end of the day you must achieve something tangible in order to feel good about yourself. And by "every day" you mean every single day — workdays, weekends, vacations. No matter how much you may feel you deserve a day of rest, if the day passes without some form of achievement, no matter how small, you will feel dissatisfied. You have an internal fire burning inside you. It pushes you to do more, to achieve more. After each accomplishment is reached, the fire dwindles for a moment, but very soon it rekindles itself, forcing you toward the next accomplishment. Your relentless need for achievement might not be logical. It might not even be focused. But it will always be with you. As an Achiever you must learn to live with this whisper of discontent. It does have its benefits. It brings you the energy you need to work long hours without burning out. It is the jolt you can always count on to get you started on new tasks, new challenges. It is the power supply that causes you to set the pace and define the levels of productivity for your workgroup. It is the theme that keeps you moving.

Scriptures that relate to the Achiever theme:

What good is it, my brothers, if someone says he has faith but does not have works? Can that faith save him? If a brother or sister has nothing to wear and has no food for the day, and one of you says to them, "Go in peace, keep warm, and eat well," but you do not give them the necessities of the body, what good is it? So also faith of itself, if it does not have works, is dead. James 2:14-17

We ask you, brothers, to respect those who are laboring among you and who are over you in the Lord and who admonish you, and to show esteem

for them with special love on account of their work. Be at peace among yourselves.
1 Thessalonians 5:12-13

The man who is slack in his work
  is own brother to the man who is destructive.
Proverbs 18:9

We earnestly desire each of you to demonstrate the same eagerness for the fulfillment of hope until the end, so that you may not become sluggish, but imitators of those who, through faith and patience, are inheriting the promises.
Hebrews 6:11-12

For further understanding of your talents, examine these five insights and select those that describe you best.

☐ You work very hard to complete each task on your "to do" list, and you always have a long list of things to do.

☐ You are busy and productive, and you derive satisfaction from your accomplishments.

☐ You have a great deal of stamina and determination to achieve your goals.

☐ Other people may criticize you, because to them you seem too driven to achieve. They may call you a "workaholic," but the truth is that you like your work, and you like to work hard.

☐ Achiever talents are valuable because they help you remain motivated to reach your goals and to push for higher and higher levels of excellence. You won't rest until you reach your most highly desired goals — and they must be *your* goals.

ACTIVATOR

"When can we start?" This is a recurring question in your life. You are impatient for action. You may concede that analysis has its uses or that debate and discussion can occasionally yield some valuable insights, but deep down you know that only action is real. Only action can make things happen. Only action leads to performance. Once a decision is made, you cannot not act. Others may worry that "there are still some things we don't know," but this doesn't seem to slow you. If the decision has been made to go across town, you know that the fastest way to get there is to go stoplight to stoplight. You are not going to sit around waiting until all the lights have turned green. Besides, in your view, action and thinking are not opposites. In fact, guided by your Activator theme, you believe that action is the best device for learning. You make a decision, you take action, you look at the result, and you learn. This learning informs your next action and your next. How can you grow if you have nothing to react to? Well, you believe you can't. You must put yourself out there. You must take the next step. It is the only way to keep your thinking fresh and informed. The bottom line is this: You know you will be judged not by what you say, not by what you think, but by what you get done. This does not frighten you. It pleases you.

Scriptures that relate to the Activator theme:

Be doers of the word and not hearers only, deluding yourselves. For if anyone is a hearer of the word and not a doer, he is like a man who looks at his own face in a mirror.
James 1:22-23

One who pays heed to the wind will not sow,
and one who watches the clouds will never reap.
Just as you know not how the breath of life
fashions the human frame in the mother's womb,
So you know not the work of God
which he is accomplishing in the universe.
In the morning sow your seed,
and at evening let not your hand be idle:
For you know not which of the two will be successful,
or whether both alike will turn out well.
Ecclesiastes 11:4-6

If you understand this, blessed are you if you do it.
John 13:17

For further understanding of your talents, examine these five insights and select those that describe you best.

- ☐ You can see how ideas can be turned into action.

- ☐ You want to do things now, rather than simply talk about doing them.

- ☐ You can be very powerful in making things happen and getting other people to take action.

- ☐ Other people may criticize you for being impatient and seeming to "run over" them. You will probably struggle with people who try to control you.

- ☐ Activator talents are valuable because they generate the energy to get things going and then done. This theme brings innovation and creative approaches to problem solving.

ADAPTABILITY

You live in the moment. You don't see the future as a fixed destination. Instead, you see it as a place that you create out of the choices that you make right now. And so you discover your future one choice at a time. This doesn't mean that you don't have plans. You probably do. But this theme of Adaptability does enable you to respond willingly to the demands of the moment even if they pull you away from your plans. Unlike some, you don't resent sudden requests or unforeseen detours. You expect them. They are inevitable. Indeed, on some level you actually look forward to them. You are, at heart, a very flexible person who can stay productive when the demands of work are pulling you in many different directions at once.

Scriptures that relate to the Adaptability theme:

Do not worry about tomorrow; tomorrow will take care of itself. Sufficient for a day is its own evil.
Matthew 6:34

And people were bringing children to him that he might touch them, but the disciples rebuked them. When Jesus saw this he became indignant and said to them, "Let the children come to me; do not prevent them, for the kingdom of God belongs to such as these. Amen, I say to you, whoever does not accept the kingdom of God like a child will not enter it." Then he embraced them and blessed them, placing his hands on them.
Mark 10:13-16

When Jesus reached the spot he looked up and spoke to him, "Zacchaeus, come down. Hurry, because I am to stay at your house today." And he hurried down and welcomed him joyfully. They all complained when they saw what was happening. "He has gone to stay at a sinner's house," they said. But Zacchaeus stood his ground and said to the Lord, "Look, sir, I am

going to give half my property to the poor, and if I have cheated anybody I will pay him back four times the amount." And Jesus said to him, "Today salvation has come to this house, because this man too is a son of Abraham; for the Son of man has come to seek out and save what was lost."
Luke 19:5-10 (NJB)

I know indeed how to live in humble circumstances; I know also how to live with abundance. In every circumstance and in all things I have learned the secret of being well fed and of going hungry, of living in abundance and of being in need. I have the strength for everything through him who empowers me.
Philippians 4:12-13

For further understanding of your talents, examine these five insights and select those that describe you best.

☐ You can modify yourself depending on the demands in your environment.

☐ You adjust to many things all day long because you live in the moment.

☐ You create and discover the future out of the choices you make right now, one choice at a time.

☐ Your "go with the flow" attitude may seem like irresponsibility to those who like structure and predictability.

☐ Adaptability talents are valuable because they allow you to keep moving forward when the unexpected happens. You can move ahead in a world of unknowns and seemingly unfair treatment when others would give up. You can deal with everything from injustices to crises and still find a way to make progress.

ANALYTICAL

Your Analytical theme challenges other people: "Prove it. Show me why what you are claiming is true." In the face of this kind of questioning some will find that their brilliant theories wither and die. For you, this is precisely the point. You do not necessarily want to destroy other people's ideas, but you do insist that their theories be sound. You see yourself as objective and dispassionate. You like data because they are value free. They have no agenda. Armed with these data, you search for patterns and connections. You want to understand how certain patterns affect one another. How do they combine? What is their outcome? Does this outcome fit with the theory being offered or the situation being confronted? These are your questions. You peel the layers back until, gradually, the root cause or causes are revealed. Others see you as logical and rigorous. Over time they will come to you in order to expose someone's "wishful thinking" or "clumsy thinking" to your refining mind. It is hoped that your analysis is never delivered too harshly. Otherwise, others may avoid you when that "wishful thinking" is their own.

Scriptures that relate to the Analytical theme:

Thomas, called Didymus, one of the Twelve, was not with them when Jesus came. So the other disciples said to him, "We have seen the Lord." But he said to them, "Unless I see the mark of the nails in his hands and put my finger into the nailmarks and put my hand into his side, I will not believe."
John 20:24-25

These Jews were more fair-minded than those in Thessalonica, for they received the word with all willingness and examined the scriptures daily to determine whether these things were so.
Acts 17:11

"Give your servant therefore an understanding heart to judge your people, that I may discern between good and evil; for who is able to judge this your great people?" The speech pleased the Lord, that Solomon had asked this thing. God said to him, "Because you have asked this thing, and have not asked for yourself long life, neither have asked riches for yourself, nor have asked the life of your enemies, but have asked for yourself understanding to discern justice; behold, I have done according to your word: behold, I have given you a wise and an understanding heart; so that there has been none like you before you, neither after you shall any arise like you."
1 Kings 3:9-12 (NJB)

For further understanding of your talents, examine these five insights and select those that describe you best.

☐ You search for the reasons why things are the way they are.

☐ You think about the factors that might affect a situation and what causes certain reactions.

☐ You are critical about why people may claim something is true and want to see the proof.

☐ Some people may reject you and your questioning ways because you insist that the facts are verifiable, theories are sound, and reasoning is logical. Some people may think you are negative or unnecessarily critical when, from your standpoint, you are simply trying to understand something.

☐ Analytical talents are valuable because they enable you to dig deep, find the root causes and effects, and then develop clear thoughts about what is true. This type of thinking helps you become clearer about what excellence is and how it can be attained.

ARRANGER

You are a conductor. When faced with a complex situation involving many factors, you enjoy managing all of the variables, aligning and realigning them until you are sure you have arranged them in the most productive configuration possible. In your mind there is nothing special about what you are doing. You are simply trying to figure out the best way to get things done. But others, lacking this theme, will be in awe of your ability. "How can you keep so many things in your head at once?" they will ask. "How can you stay so flexible, so willing to shelve well-laid plans in favor of some brand-new configuration that has just occurred to you?" But you cannot imagine behaving in any other way. You are a shining example of effective flexibility, whether you are changing travel schedules at the last minute because a better fare has popped up or mulling over just the right combination of people and resources to accomplish a new project. From the mundane to the complex, you are always looking for the perfect configuration. Of course, you are at your best in dynamic situations. Confronted with the unexpected, some complain that plans devised with such care cannot be changed, while others take refuge in the existing rules or procedures. You don't do either. Instead, you jump into the confusion, devising new options, hunting for new paths of least resistance, and figuring out new partnerships — because, after all, there might just be a better way.

Scriptures that relate to the Arranger theme:

Plans fail when there is no counsel,
but they succeed when counselors are many.
Proverbs 15:22

What are humans that you are mindful of them,
  mere mortals that you care for them?
Yet you have made them little less than a god,
  crowned them with glory and honor.
You have given them rule over the works of your hands,
  put all things at their feet:
Psalm 8:5-7

For further understanding of your talents, examine these five insights and select those that describe you best.

☐ You are highly organized and highly flexible.

☐ You can get a lot done, even though you usually have many projects going at the same time.

☐ You enjoy coordinating all of the complex factors that go into making a project successful.

☐ Some people who like to do things by rules and procedures may find your ways chaotic. They may think that your effectiveness is mystery or pure luck.

☐ Arranger talents are valuable because they help you keep looking for the right combinations of people and resources to complete projects successfully.

BELIEF

If you possess a strong Belief theme, you have certain core values that are enduring. These values vary from one person to another, but ordinarily your Belief theme causes you to be family-oriented, altruistic, even spiritual, and to value responsibility and high ethics — both in yourself and others. These core values affect your behavior in many ways. They give your life meaning and satisfaction; in your view, success is more than money and prestige. They provide you with direction, guiding you through the temptations and distractions of life toward a consistent set of priorities. This consistency is the foundation for all your relationships. Your friends call you dependable. "I know where you stand," they say. Your Belief makes you easy to trust. It also demands that you find work that meshes with your values. Your work must be meaningful; it must matter to you. And guided by your Belief theme it will matter only if it gives you a chance to live out your values.

Scriptures that relate to the Belief theme:

"If it does not please you to serve the LORD, decide today whom you will serve, the gods your fathers served beyond the River or the gods of the Amorites in whose country you are dwelling. As for me and my household, we will serve the LORD."
Joshua 24:15

Whatever you do, do from the heart, as for the Lord and not for others, knowing that you will receive from the Lord the due payment of the inheritance; be slaves of the Lord Christ.
Colossians 3:23-24

Then he said to Thomas, "Put your finger here and see my hands, and bring your hand and put it into my side, and do not be unbelieving, but believe." Thomas answered and said to him, "My Lord and my God!" Jesus said to him, "Have you come to believe because you have seen me? Blessed are those who have not seen and have believed."
John 20:27-29

For further understanding of your talents, examine these five insights and select those that describe you best.

- ☐ You have core values that are unchanging. You may conflict with people who oppose or don't value your beliefs.

- ☐ You have deeply held ideas about what is, what should be, and the purpose of your life.

- ☐ You will become energetic about a task, role, or position that promotes one of your deeply held beliefs.

- ☐ Some people may think you are rigid or contrary because of your strongly held beliefs.

- ☐ Belief talents are valuable because they produce the motivation for you to work hard, excel, and achieve, as long as achieving is consistent with your values and beliefs. Your set of beliefs does more than energize you — it is the basis for developing a meaningful life.

COMMAND

Command leads you to take charge. Unlike some people, you feel no discomfort with imposing your views on others. On the contrary, once your opinion is formed, you need to share it with others. Once your goal is set, you feel restless until you have aligned others with you. You are not frightened by confrontation; rather, you know that confrontation is the first step toward resolution. Whereas others may avoid facing up to life's unpleasantness, you feel compelled to present the facts or the truth, no matter how unpleasant it may be. You need things to be clear between people and challenge them to be clear-eyed and honest. You push them to take risks. You may even intimidate them. And while some may resent this, labeling you opinionated, they often willingly hand you the reins. People are drawn toward those who take a stance and ask them to move in a certain direction. Therefore, people will be drawn to you. You have presence. You have Command.

Scriptures that relate to the Command theme:

He made a whip out of cords and drove them all out of the temple area, with the sheep and oxen, and spilled the coins of the money-changers and overturned their tables, and to those who sold doves he said, "Take these out of here, and stop making my Father's house a marketplace." His disciples recalled the words of scripture, "Zeal for your house will consume me."
John 2:15-17

Therefore, putting away falsehood, speak the truth, each one to his neighbor, for we are members one of another.
Ephesians 4:25

David said to Saul, "Let no one be discouraged on his account; your servant will go and fight this Philistine." Saul said to David, "You cannot go and fight the Philistine; you are only a boy and he has been a warrior since his youth." David said to Saul, "Your servant used to look after the sheep for his father and whenever a lion or a bear came and took a sheep from the flock, I used to follow it up, lay into it and snatch the sheep out of its jaws. If it turned on me, I would seize it by the beard and batter it to death. Your servant has killed both lion and bear, and this uncircumcised Philistine will end up like one of them for having challenged the armies of the living God." "Yahweh," David went on, "who delivered me from the claws of lion and bear, will deliver me from the clutches of this Philistine." Then Saul said to David, "Go, and Yahweh be with you!"

1 Samuel 17:32-37 (NJB)

For further understanding of your talents, examine these five insights and select those that describe you best.

☐ You see what needs to be done, and you are willing to say so.

☐ You are willing to go into a confrontation and argue because you know that what is right will prevail, and confrontations often help get things moving.

☐ You can jump into a conflict, crisis, or emergency and take charge of the situation.

☐ Other people may be threatened, offended, or put off by the power you can command, but most wish they had some of your talents.

☐ Command talents are valuable because they help you have a positive impact on other people. You can help people and entire organizations get through difficult times and make substantive changes in the midst of chaos.

COMMUNICATION

You like to explain, to describe, to host, to speak in public, and to write. This is your Communication theme at work. Ideas are a dry beginning. Events are static. You feel a need to bring them to life, to energize them, to make them exciting and vivid. And so you turn events into stories and practice telling them. You take the dry idea and enliven it with images and examples and metaphors. You believe that most people have a very short attention span. They are bombarded by information, but very little of it survives. You want your information — whether an idea, an event, a product's features and benefits, a discovery, or a lesson — to survive. You want to divert their attention toward you and then capture it, lock it in. This is what drives your hunt for the perfect phrase. This is what draws you toward dramatic words and powerful word combinations. This is why people like to listen to you. Your word pictures pique their interest, sharpen their world, and inspire them to act.

Scriptures that relate to the Communication theme:

When Jesus finished these words, the crowds were astonished at his teaching, for he taught them as one having authority, and not as their scribes.
Matthew 7:28-29

All these things Jesus spoke to the crowds in parables. He spoke to them only in parables...
Matthew 13:34

Besides being wise, Qoheleth taught the people knowledge, and weighed, scrutinized and arranged many proverbs. Qoheleth sought to find pleasing

sayings, and to write down true sayings with precision. The sayings of the wise are like goads; like fixed spikes are the topics given by one collector.
Ecclesiastes 12:9-11

But how can they call on him in whom they have not believed? And how can they believe in him of whom they have not heard? And how can they hear without someone to preach? And how can people preach unless they are sent? As it is written, "How beautiful are the feet of those who bring (the) good news!"
Romans 10:14-15

For further understanding of your talents, examine these five insights and select those that describe you best.

☐ You like to talk, and you are good at it.

☐ You can explain things and make them clear.

☐ You may have an ability to tell particularly captivating stories by constructing mental images in the minds of others.

☐ You may have been criticized because you like to talk a lot.

☐ Communication talents are valuable because your abilities in this area enable you to reach out and connect with people. Your story-telling ability builds images in the minds of others and makes you a powerful person as you connect and bond with people.

COMPETITION

Competition is rooted in comparison. When you look at the world, you are instinctively aware of other people's performance. Their performance is the ultimate yardstick. No matter how hard you tried, no matter how worthy your intentions, if you reached your goal but did not outperform your peers, the achievement feels hollow. Like all competitors, you need other people. You need to compare. If you can compare, you can compete, and if you can compete, you can win. And when you win, there is no feeling quite like it. You like measurement because it facilitates comparisons. You like other competitors because they invigorate you. You like contests because they must produce a winner. You particularly like contests where you know you have the inside track to be the winner. Although you are gracious to your fellow competitors and even stoic in defeat, you don't compete for the fun of competing. You compete to win. Over time you will come to avoid contests where winning seems unlikely.

Scriptures that relate to the Competition theme:

You belong to God, children, and you have conquered them, for the one who is in you is greater than the one who is in the world.
1 John 4:4

Do you not know that the runners in the stadium all run in the race, but only one wins the prize? Run so as to win. Every athlete exercises discipline in every way. They do it to win a perishable crown, but we an imperishable one. Thus I do not run aimlessly; I do not fight as if I were shadowboxing. No, I drive my body and train it, for fear that, after having preached to others, I myself should be disqualified.
1 Corinthians 9:24-27

A champion stepped out from the Philistine ranks; his name was Goliath, from Gath; he was six cubits and one span tall. On his head was a bronze helmet and he wore a breastplate of scale-armour; the breastplate weighed five thousand shekels of bronze. He had bronze greaves on his legs and a bronze scimitar slung across his shoulders. The shaft of his spear was like a weaver's beam, and the head of his spear weighed six hundred shekels of iron. A shield-bearer walked in front of him. Taking position in front of the Israelite lines, he shouted, "Why have you come out to range yourselves for battle? Am I not a Philistine and are you not Saul's lackeys? Choose a man and let him come down to me. If he can fight it out with me and kill me, we will be your servants; but if I can beat him and kill him, you become our servants and serve us." The Philistine then said, "I challenge the ranks of Israel today. Give me a man and we will fight it out!"
1 Samuel 17:4-10 (NJB)

And when this which is corruptible clothes itself with incorruptibility and this which is mortal clothes itself with immortality, then the word that is written shall come about:
    "Death is swallowed up in victory.
    Where, O death, is your victory?
    Where, O death, is your sting?"
The sting of death is sin, and the power of sin is the law. But thanks be to God who gives us the victory through our Lord Jesus Christ.
1 Corinthians 15:54-57

For further understanding of your talents, examine these five insights and select those that describe you best.

☐ You want to win, which usually means outperforming others.

☐ You will work very hard to excel past others.

☐ You constantly compare yourself and your performance to other people and their performances.

☐ You may not be willing to try something if you think you can't win. Other people may consider your competitiveness inappropriate and therefore push you away, reject you, or accuse you of being arrogant.

☐ Competition talents are valuable because through them you will influence and even push people in your group to achieve more than other groups. You bring energy to a group and can energize others to move to higher levels of excellence.

CONNECTEDNESS

Things happen for a reason. You are sure of it. You are sure of it because in your soul you know that we are all connected. Yes, we are individuals, responsible for our own judgments and in possession of our own free will, but nonetheless we are part of something larger. Some may call it the collective unconscious. Others may label it spirit or life force. But whatever your word of choice, you gain confidence from knowing that we are not isolated from one another or from the earth and the life on it. This feeling of Connectedness implies certain responsibilities. If we are all part of a larger picture, then we must not harm others because we will be harming ourselves. We must not exploit because we will be exploiting ourselves. Your awareness of these responsibilities creates your value system. You are considerate, caring, and accepting. Certain of the unity of humankind, you are a bridge builder for people of different cultures. Sensitive to the invisible hand, you can give others comfort that there is a purpose beyond our humdrum lives. The exact articles of your faith will depend on your upbringing and your culture, but your faith is strong. It sustains you and your close friends in the face of life's mysteries.

Scriptures that relate to the Connectedness theme:

We know that all things work for good for those who love God, who are called according to his purpose.
Romans 8:28

Ask and it will be given to you; seek and you will find; knock and the door will be opened to you. For everyone who asks, receives; and the one who seeks, finds; and to the one who knocks, the door will be opened.
Matthew 7:7-8

But as it is, God placed the parts, each one of them, in the body as he intended. If they were all one part, where would the body be? But as it is, there are many parts, yet one body. The eye cannot say to the hand, "I do not need you," nor again the head to the feet, "I do not need you." ... If (one) part suffers, all the parts suffer with it; if one part is honored, all the parts share its joy. Now you are Christ's body, and individually parts of it.
1 Corinthians 12:18-21, 26-27

I, the prisoner in the Lord, urge you therefore to lead a life worthy of the vocation to which you were called. With all humility and gentleness, and with patience, support each other in love. Take every care to preserve the unity of the Spirit by the peace that binds you together. There is one Body, one Spirit, just as one hope is the goal of your calling by God. There is one Lord, one faith, one baptism, and one God and Father of all, over all, through all and within all.
Ephesians 4:1-6 (NJB)

For further understanding of your talents, examine these five insights and select those that describe you best.

☐ You see that all things happen for a reason. All things are working together in a purposeful manner.

☐ You feel connected to life itself. Therefore, you feel a responsibility to be considerate, caring, and accepting toward others.

☐ You are a bridge builder for people from all backgrounds to come together and develop a faith that goes beyond themselves.

☐ When people and the world seem fractured, broken, and isolated, you become discouraged and sometimes distressed. For this reason, some may perceive you as too naïve or fragile.

☐ Connectedness talents are valuable because they provide you with conviction and faith that sustain and encourage you and your friends in difficult times. You believe that there's a plan, a design, and a power beyond the visible world that provide meaning, comfort, and confidence. Your Connectedness gives you hope and helps you to achieve your ultimate goals.

CONSISTENCY

Balance is important to you. You are keenly aware of the need to treat people the same, no matter what their station in life, so you do not want to see the scales tipped too far in any one person's favor. In your view this leads to selfishness and individualism. It leads to a world where some people gain an unfair advantage because of their connections or their background or their greasing of the wheels. This is truly offensive to you. You see yourself as a guardian against it. In direct contrast to this world of special favors, you believe that people function best in a consistent environment where the rules are clear and are applied to everyone equally. This is an environment where people know what is expected. It is predictable and evenhanded. It is fair. Here each person has an even chance to show his or her worth.

Scriptures that relate to the Consistency theme:

My brothers, show no partiality as you adhere to the faith in our glorious Lord Jesus Christ…However, if you fulfill the royal law according to the scripture, "You shall love your neighbor as yourself," you are doing well. But if you show partiality, you commit sin, and are convicted by the law as transgressors.
James 2:1, 8-9

…for he makes his sun rise on the bad and the good, and causes rain to fall on the just and the unjust.
Matthew 5:45

For by the grace given to me I tell everyone among you not to think of himself more highly than one ought to think, but to think soberly, each according to the measure of faith that God has apportioned.
Romans 12:3

For further understanding of your talents, examine these five insights and select those that describe you best.

- ☐ You try to treat everyone consistently by having clear rules and applying them to everyone in the same way.

- ☐ You are offended when some people gain an advantage because of their connections or the games they play.

- ☐ You believe that people work best in a consistent environment where the rules apply to everyone equally, and you work to create this type of environment.

- ☐ While you may see yourself as a guardian of what is right and a warrior against special treatment, some people may reject you for assuming that responsibility.

- ☐ Consistency talents are valuable because you can more easily recognize inconsistencies, and you can readily suggest changes that can create a more equitable world.

CONTEXT

You look back. You look back because that is where the answers lie. You look back to understand the present. From your vantage point the present is unstable, a confusing clamor of competing voices. It is only by casting your mind back to an earlier time, a time when the plans were being drawn up, that the present regains its stability. The earlier time was a simpler time. It was a time of blueprints. As you look back, you begin to see these blueprints emerge. You realize what the initial intentions were. These blueprints or intentions have since become so embellished that they are almost unrecognizable, but now this Context theme reveals them again. This understanding brings you confidence. No longer disoriented, you make better decisions because you sense the underlying structure. You become a better partner because you understand how your colleagues came to be who they are. And counterintuitively you become wiser about the future because you saw its seeds being sown in the past. Faced with new people and new situations, it will take you a little time to orient yourself, but you must give yourself this time. You must discipline yourself to ask the questions and allow the blueprints to emerge because no matter what the situation, if you haven't seen the blueprints, you will have less confidence in your decisions.

Scriptures that relate to the Context theme:

"But take care, as you value your lives! Do not forget the things which you yourselves have seen, or let them slip from your heart as long as you live; teach them, rather, to your children and to your children's children. The day you stood at Horeb in the presence of Yahweh your God, Yahweh said to me, 'Summon the people to me; I want them to hear me speaking, so that

they will learn to fear me all the days they live on earth, and teach this to their children.'"
Deuteronomy 4:9-10 (NJB)

In times past, God spoke in partial and various ways to our ancestors through the prophets; in these last days, he spoke to us through a son, whom he made heir of all things and through whom he created the universe,
Hebrews 1:1-2

Joshua said to them: "Go to the bed of the Jordan in front of the ark of the LORD, *your God; lift to your shoulders one stone apiece, so that they will equal in number the tribes of the Israelites. In the future, these are to be a sign among you. When your children ask you what these stones mean to you, you shall answer them, 'The waters of the Jordan ceased to flow before the ark of the covenant of the* LORD *when it crossed the Jordan.' Thus these stones are to serve as a perpetual memorial to the Israelites."*
Joshua 4:5-7

What now is has already been; what is to be, already is; and God restores what would otherwise be displaced.
Ecclesiastes 3:15

"Do not think that I have come to abolish the law or the prophets. I have come not to abolish but to fulfill."
Matthew 5:17

For further understanding of your talents, examine these five insights and select those that describe you best.

☐ You look to the past to understand the present.

☐ You see patterns that emerge from studying what happened before.

☐ You learn best when you place what is to be learned into the context of other important dynamics and the history of what you are learning.

☐ You may feel disoriented when you can't see patterns stemming from the past. Others may become impatient with you as you strive to build an understanding of life's many complexities. You may be perceived as "slow" because you want to understand how we got to where we are.

☐ Context talents are valuable because they provide perspective that enhances your ability and confidence in making decisions and action planning.

DELIBERATIVE

You are careful. You are vigilant. You are a private person. You know that the world is an unpredictable place. Everything may seem in order, but beneath the surface you sense the many risks. Rather than denying these risks, you draw each one out into the open. Then each risk can be identified, assessed, and ultimately reduced. Thus, you are a fairly serious person who approaches life with a certain reserve. For example, you like to plan ahead so as to anticipate what might go wrong. You select your friends cautiously and keep your own counsel when the conversation turns to personal matters. You are careful not to give too much praise and recognition, lest it be misconstrued. If some people don't like you because you are not as effusive as others, then so be it. For you, life is not a popularity contest. Life is something of a minefield. Others can run through it recklessly if they so choose, but you take a different approach. You identify the dangers, weigh their relative impact, and then place your feet deliberately. You walk with care.

Scriptures that relate to the Deliberative theme:

Watch carefully then how you live, not as foolish persons but as wise, making the most of the opportunity, because the days are evil.
Ephesians 5:15-16

Know this, my dear brothers: everyone should be quick to hear, slow to speak, slow to wrath, for the wrath of a man does not accomplish the righteousness of God.
James 1:19-20

Which of you wishing to construct a tower does not first sit down and calculate the cost to see if there is enough for its completion? Otherwise, after laying the foundation and finding himself unable to finish the work

the onlookers should laugh at him and say, "This one began to build but did not have the resources to finish."
Luke 14:28-30

For further understanding of your talents, examine these five insights and select those that describe you best.

☐ You take great care as you consider options, thinking through the pros and cons of each alternative.

☐ To you, making the correct decision is more important than the time it takes to do so.

☐ You make very good decisions. In fact, you would change few of your choices or decisions.

☐ You may exhaust yourself and others as you make your decisions cautiously and slowly. You always think about the risks and what might go wrong. Therefore, some may falsely judge you as a pessimist. You may even be falsely categorized as less intelligent when in fact you are doing some very deep thinking.

☐ Deliberative talents are valuable because they enable you to eliminate or reduce errors by thoroughly considering each option. Though this may add time to the decision-making process, the results are usually worth the wait.

DEVELOPER

You see the potential in others. Very often, in fact, potential is all you see. In your view no individual is fully formed. On the contrary, each individual is a work in progress, alive with possibilities. And you are drawn toward people for this very reason. When you interact with others, your goal is to help them experience success. You look for ways to challenge them. You devise interesting experiences that can stretch them and help them grow. And all the while you are on the lookout for the signs of growth — a new behavior learned or modified, a slight improvement in a skill, a glimpse of excellence or of "flow" where previously there were only halting steps. For you these small increments — invisible to some — are clear signs of potential being realized. These signs of growth in others are your fuel. They bring you strength and satisfaction. Over time many will seek you out for help and encouragement because on some level they know that your helpfulness is both genuine and fulfilling to you.

Scriptures that relate to the Developer theme:

The news of them came to the ears of the church in Jerusalem and they sent Barnabas out to Antioch. There he was glad to see for himself that God had given grace, and he urged them all to remain faithful to the Lord with heartfelt devotion; for he was a good man, filled with the Holy Spirit and with faith. And a large number of people were won over to the Lord. Barnabas then left for Tarsus to look for Saul, and when he found him he brought him to Antioch. And it happened that they stayed together in that church a whole year, instructing a large number of people. It was at Antioch that the disciples were first called "Christians."
Acts 11:22-26 (NJB)

I give thanks to my God at every remembrance of you, praying always with joy in my every prayer for all of you, because of your partnership for the gospel from the first day until now. I am confident of this, that the one who began a good work in you will continue to complete it until the day of Christ Jesus.
Philippians 1:3-6

...we were gentle among you, as a nursing mother cares for her children. With such affection for you, we were determined to share with you not only the gospel of God, but our very selves as well, so dearly beloved had you become to us ...As you know, we treated each one of you as a father treats his children, exhorting and encouraging you and insisting that you conduct yourselves as worthy of the God who calls you into his kingdom and glory.
1 Thessalonians 2:7-8, 11-12

And what you heard from me through many witnesses entrust to faithful people who will have the ability to teach others as well.
2 Timothy 2:2

For further understanding of your talents, examine these five insights and select those that describe you best.

☐ You can see how other people can move, change, grow, and develop for the better.

☐ You love to see others make progress, and you will notice even the slightest progress.

☐ When you are a part of someone's development, it is the best experience in the world for you.

☐ Other people may not be as interested or ready to make the progress that you want them to make. Therefore, you may become frustrated when people don't want to improve, and you may feel frustrated or hurt when other people push you away because they feel pressured to improve.

☐ Developer talents are valuable because they help you see the potential in others and move them in that direction. People usually grow and improve in the presence of a developer. When you fully apply your Developer talents, it is as if you are educating, counseling, and encouraging people all the time.

DISCIPLINE

Your world needs to be predictable. It needs to be ordered and planned. So you instinctively impose structure on your world. You set up routines. You focus on timelines and deadlines. You break long-term projects into a series of specific short-term plans, and you work through each plan diligently. You are not necessarily neat and clean, but you do need precision. Faced with the inherent messiness of life, you want to feel in control. The routines, the timelines, the structure, all of these help create this feeling of control. Lacking this theme of Discipline, others may sometimes resent your need for order, but there need not be conflict. You must understand that not everyone feels your urge for predictability; they have other ways of getting things done. Likewise, you can help them understand and even appreciate your need for structure. Your dislike of surprises, your impatience with errors, your routines, and your detail orientation don't need to be misinterpreted as controlling behaviors that box people in. Rather, these behaviors can be understood as your instinctive method for maintaining your progress and your productivity in the face of life's many distractions.

Scriptures that relate to the Discipline theme:

…but everything must be done properly and in order.
1 Corinthians 14:40

He had successfully committed to writing the exact specifications of the pattern, because the hand of the LORD was upon him.
1 Chronicles 28:19

The plans of the diligent are sure of profit,
    but all rash haste leads certainly to poverty.
Proverbs 21:5

For further understanding of your talents, examine these five insights and select those that describe you best.

☐ You find ways to organize yourself to get things done on time.

☐ You tend to place yourself in productive environments.

☐ You create order and structure where it is needed.

☐ Some people may label you as compulsive or a control freak because of your ability to discipline yourself and structure your world. But these attributes make you productive — usually more so than your critics.

☐ Discipline talents are valuable because they make you efficient *and* effective. First, they motivate you to organize tasks. Then, they keep you motivated to complete those tasks.

EMPATHY

You can sense the emotions of those around you. You can feel what they are feeling as though their feelings are your own. Intuitively, you are able to see the world through their eyes and share their perspective. You do not necessarily agree with each person's perspective. You do not necessarily feel pity for each person's predicament — this would be sympathy, not Empathy. You do not necessarily condone the choices each person makes, but you do understand. This instinctive ability to understand is powerful. You hear the unvoiced questions. You anticipate the need. Where others grapple for words, you seem to find the right words and the right tone. You help people find the right phrases to express their feelings — to themselves as well as to others. You help them give voice to their emotional life. For all these reasons other people are drawn to you.

Scriptures that relate to the Empathy theme:

When Jesus saw her weeping and the Jews who had come with her weeping, he became perturbed and deeply troubled, and said, "Where have you laid him?" They said to him, "Sir, come and see." And Jesus wept.
John 11:33-35

Rejoice with those who rejoice, weep with those who weep.
Romans 12:15

Now there was a woman suffering from a haemorrhage for the past twelve years, whom no one had been able to cure. She came up behind him and touched the fringe of his cloak; and the haemorrhage stopped at that very moment. Jesus said, "Who was it that touched me?" When they all denied it, Peter said, "Master, it is the crowds round you, pushing." But Jesus said, "Somebody touched me. I felt that power had gone out from me." Seeing

herself discovered, the woman came forward trembling, and falling at his feet explained in front of all the people why she had touched him and how she had been cured at that very moment. "My daughter," he said, "your faith has saved you; go in peace."
Luke 8:43-48

For further understanding of your talents, examine these five insights and select those that describe you best.

☐ You can sense what it feels like to be someone else.

☐ You can pick up on the pain and joy of others — sometimes before they can express it. Other people feel heard by you and experience your compassion.

☐ Because you can quickly understand others, people are drawn to you when they have a need or a problem, especially in relationships.

☐ Your Empathy can be challenging because you may become overwhelmed with all of the emotions you can pick up in a day. Roles and relationships in which people project their negative emotions your way are hard on you. You can become exhausted from the emotions you pick up from others.

☐ Empathy talents are valuable because they enable you to form very close, supportive relationships in which you help and encourage others.

FOCUS

"Where am I headed?" you ask yourself. You ask this question every day. Guided by this theme of Focus, you need a clear destination. Lacking one, your life and your work can quickly become frustrating. And so each year, each month, and even each week you set goals. These goals then serve as your compass, helping you determine priorities and make the necessary corrections to get back on course. Your Focus is powerful because it forces you to filter; you instinctively evaluate whether or not a particular action will help you move toward your goal. Those that don't are ignored. In the end, then, your Focus forces you to be efficient. Naturally, the flip side of this is that it causes you to become impatient with delays, obstacles, and even tangents, no matter how intriguing they appear to be. This makes you an extremely valuable team member. When others start to wander down other avenues, you bring them back to the main road. Your Focus reminds everyone that if something is not helping you move toward your destination, then it is not important. And if it is not important, then it is not worth your time. You keep everyone on point.

Scriptures that relate to the Focus theme:

When the days for his being taken up were fulfilled, he resolutely determined to journey to Jerusalem...
Luke 9:51

Not that I have secured it already, nor yet reached my goal, but I am still pursuing it in the attempt to take hold of the prize for which Christ Jesus took hold of me. Brothers, I do not reckon myself as having taken hold of it; I can only say that forgetting all that lies behind me, and straining forward

to what lies in front, I am racing towards the finishing-point to win the prize of God's heavenly call in Christ Jesus.
Philippians 3:12-14 (NJB)

Therefore, since we are surrounded by so great a cloud of witnesses, let us rid ourselves of every burden and sin that clings to us and persevere in running the race that lies before us while keeping our eyes fixed on Jesus, the leader and perfecter of faith. For the sake of the joy that lay before him he endured the cross, despising its shame, and has taken his seat at the right of the throne of God.
Hebrews 12:1-2

For further understanding of your talents, examine these five insights and select those that describe you best.

☐ You can take a direction, follow through, and make the necessary corrections to stay on track.

☐ You prioritize your life and tasks, and then you take action.

☐ You set goals that keep you effective and efficient.

☐ You become frustrated when you can't determine what a group is trying to do. Likewise, your life and work become frustrating when your goals are unclear.

☐ Focus talents are valuable because you can quickly evaluate, determine priorities, and get yourself and groups on course quickly. Your Focus motivates you to be efficient. You get a lot done because you don't get easily distracted.

FUTURISTIC

"Wouldn't it be great if…" You are the kind of person who loves to peer over the horizon. The future fascinates you. As if it were projected on the wall, you see in detail what the future might hold, and this detailed picture keeps pulling you forward, into tomorrow. While the exact content of the picture will depend on your other strengths and interests — a better product, a better team, a better life, or a better world — it will always be inspirational to you. You are a dreamer who sees visions of what could be and who cherishes those visions. When the present proves too frustrating and the people around you too pragmatic, you conjure up your visions of the future and they energize you. They can energize others, too. In fact, very often people look to you to describe your visions of the future. They want a picture that can raise their sights and thereby their spirits. You can paint it for them. Practice. Choose your words carefully. Make the picture as vivid as possible. People will want to latch on to the hope you bring.

Scriptures that relate to the Futuristic theme:

Without prophecy the people become demoralized…
Proverbs 29:18

*Then afterward I will pour out
    my spirit upon all mankind.
Your sons and daughters shall prophesy,
    your old men shall dream dreams,
    your young men shall see visions;*
Joel 3:1

Now Joseph had a dream, and he repeated it to his brothers, who then hated him more than ever. "Listen", he said, "to the dream I had. We were binding sheaves in the field, when my sheaf suddenly rose and stood upright, and then your sheaves gathered round and bowed to my sheaf." "So you want to be king over us," his brothers retorted, "you want to lord it over us?" And they hated him even more, on account of his dreams and of what he said.
Genesis 37:5-8 (NJB)

I consider that the sufferings of this present time are as nothing compared with the glory to be revealed for us. For creation awaits with eager expectation the revelation of the children of God; for creation was made subject to futility, not of its own accord but because of the one who subjected it, in hope that creation itself would be set free from slavery to corruption and share in the glorious freedom of the children of God.
Romans 8:18-21

For I know well the plans I have in mind for you, says the LORD, plans for your welfare, not for woe! plans to give you a future full of hope.
Jeremiah 29:11

For further understanding of your talents, examine these five insights and select those that describe you best.

☐ You are fascinated by the future, and you usually see the future positively.

☐ You can see in detail what the future might hold.

☐ You can energize yourself and others by your vision of what could be. You can clearly see possibilities.

☐ Others may dismiss you as a dreamer. You may become frustrated by present circumstances and discouraged by highly pragmatic people who can't or won't see the possibilities in the future that are so clear to you.

☐ Futuristic talents are valuable because your vision raises others' sights and focuses their energies.

HARMONY

You look for areas of agreement. In your view there is little to be gained from conflict and friction, so you seek to hold them to a minimum. When you know that the people around you hold differing views, you try to find the common ground. You try to steer them away from confrontation and toward harmony. In fact, harmony is one of your guiding values. You can't quite believe how much time is wasted by people trying to impose their views on others. Wouldn't we all be more productive if we kept our opinions in check and instead looked for consensus and support? You believe we would, and you live by that belief. When others are sounding off about their goals, their claims, and their fervently held opinions, you hold your peace. When others strike out in a direction, you will willingly, in the service of harmony, modify your own objectives to merge with theirs (as long as their basic values do not clash with yours). When others start to argue about their pet theory or concept, you steer clear of the debate, preferring to talk about practical, down-to-earth matters on which you can all agree. In your view we are all in the same boat, and we need this boat to get where we are going. It is a good boat. There is no need to rock it just to show that you can.

Scriptures that relate to the Harmony theme:

Have the same regard for one another…
Romans 12:16

Blessed are the peacemakers,
   for they will be called children of God.
Matthew 5:9

I urge you, brothers, in the name of our Lord Jesus Christ, that all of you agree in what you say, and that there be no divisions among you, but that you be united in the same mind and in the same purpose.
1 Corinthians 1:10

How good it is, how pleasant,
*   where the people dwell as one!*
Psalm 133:1

The start of strife is like the opening of a dam;
*   therefore, check a quarrel before it begins!*
Proverbs 17:14

For further understanding of your talents, examine these five insights and select those that describe you best.

☐ You want peace, and you try to bring people together.

☐ You can see points that people have in common, even when they are in conflict.

☐ You seek to help individuals, families, and organizations work together.

☐ Some people may criticize you or misunderstand you. They may say that you lack courage. You too may see your desire for harmony as only an avoidance of conflict.

☐ Harmony talents are valuable because you see what people have in common and try to help them interact on the basis of shared points of view. This binds people to you and helps groups come together. Groups, organizations, and teams function better and achieve more because of what you do to bring people together.

IDEATION

You are fascinated by ideas. What is an idea? An idea is a concept, the best explanation of the most events. You are delighted when you discover beneath the complex surface an elegantly simple concept to explain why things are the way they are. An idea is a connection. Yours is the kind of mind that is always looking for connections, and so you are intrigued when seemingly disparate phenomena can be linked by an obscure connection. An idea is a new perspective on familiar challenges. You revel in taking the world we all know and turning it around so we can view it from a strange but strangely enlightening angle. You love all these ideas because they are profound, because they are novel, because they are clarifying, because they are contrary, because they are bizarre. For all these reasons you derive a jolt of energy whenever a new idea occurs to you. Others may label you creative or original or conceptual or even smart. Perhaps you are all of these. Who can be sure? What you are sure of is that ideas are thrilling. And on most days this is enough.

Scriptures that relate to the Ideation theme:

Lo, I am about to create new heavens
    and a new earth;
The things of the past shall not be remembered
    or come to mind.
Instead, there shall always be rejoicing and happiness
    in what I create;
For I create Jerusalem to be a joy
    and its people to be a delight;
Isaiah 65:17-18

Do not conform yourself to this age but be transformed by the renewal of your mind, that you may discern what is the will of God, what is good and pleasing and perfect.
Romans 12:2

"Worthy are you, Lord our God,
to receive glory and honor and power,
for you created all things;
because of your will they came to be and were created."
Revelation 4:11

For further understanding of your talents, examine these five insights and select those that describe you best.

☐ You are a creative person, and you appreciate originality.

☐ You like free-thinking experiences such as brainstorming and discussion groups.

☐ You love new ideas and concepts.

☐ At times, it may seem like you get lost in the world of ideas, and others may think you are a little "spacey."

☐ Ideation talents are valuable because they enable you to look for new connections and generate new insights when things don't make sense. You are able to help others take the world they know and turn it around so that they can see it from a new point of view.

INCLUDER

"Stretch the circle wider." This is the philosophy around which you orient your life. You want to include people and make them feel part of the group. In direct contrast to those who are drawn only to exclusive groups, you actively avoid those groups that exclude others. You want to expand the group so that as many people as possible can benefit from its support. You hate the sight of someone on the outside looking in. You want to draw them in so that they can feel the warmth of the group. You are an instinctively accepting person. Regardless of race or sex or nationality or personality or faith, you cast few judgments. Judgments can hurt a person's feelings. Why do that if you don't have to? Your accepting nature does not necessarily rest on a belief that each of us is different and that one should respect these differences. Rather, it rests on your conviction that fundamentally we are all the same. We are all equally important. Thus, no one should be ignored. Each of us should be included. It is the least we all deserve.

Scriptures that relate to the Includer theme:

There is neither Jew nor Greek, there is neither slave nor free person, there is not male and female; for you are all one in Christ Jesus.
Galatians 3:28

For God so loved the world that he gave his only Son, so that everyone who believes in him might not perish but might have eternal life.
John 3:16

So if you regard me as a partner, welcome him as you would me.
Philemon 17

Welcome one another, then, as Christ welcomed you, for the glory of God.
Romans 15:7

For further understanding of your talents, examine these five insights and select those that describe you best.

☐ You notice people who feel like outsiders or who feel unappreciated.

☐ You are not content when people are left out, so you try to reach out to the "outsiders," and you try to bring them in.

☐ People see you as accepting and sense that you want them to be included.

☐ In your attempts to include others, you may be rejected by the very people you try to include. You may have to confront your own fears as you seek to include those who may reject you. You may also have to deal with people who misunderstand your actions and yet do nothing to reach out to those who feel left out.

☐ Includer talents are valuable because they enable you to help individuals, groups, organizations, and communities to be unified and effective. People who have felt rejected will appreciate your efforts.

INDIVIDUALIZATION

Your Individualization theme leads you to be intrigued by the unique qualities of each person. You are impatient with generalizations or "types" because you don't want to obscure what is special and distinct about each person. Instead, you focus on the differences between individuals. You instinctively observe each person's style, each person's motivation, how each thinks, and how each builds relationships. You hear the one-of-a-kind stories in each person's life. This theme explains why you pick your friends just the right birthday gift, why you know that one person prefers praise in public and another detests it, and why you tailor your teaching style to accommodate one person's need to be shown and another's desire to "figure it out as I go." Because you are such a keen observer of other people's strengths, you can draw out the best in each person. This Individualization theme also helps you build productive teams. While some search around for the perfect team "structure" or "process," you know instinctively that the secret to great teams is casting by individual strengths so that everyone can do a lot of what they do well.

Scriptures that relate to the Individualization theme:

Even the hairs of your head have all been counted. Do not be afraid. You are worth more than many sparrows.
Luke 12:7

LORD, you have probed me, you know me:
    you know when I sit and stand;
    you understand my thoughts from afar.
My travels and my rest you mark;
    with all my ways you are familiar.
Psalm 139:1-3

But the Lord *said to Samuel: "Do not judge from his appearance or from his lofty stature, because I have rejected him. Not as man sees does God see, because man sees the appearance but the* Lord *looks into the heart."*
1 Samuel 16:7

Then he summoned his twelve disciples and gave them authority over unclean spirits to drive them out and to cure every disease and every illness. The names of the twelve apostles are these: first, Simon called Peter, and his brother Andrew; James, the son of Zebedee, and his brother John; Philip and Bartholomew, Thomas and Matthew the tax collector; James, the son of Alphaeus, and Thaddeus; Simon the Cananean, and Judas Iscariot who betrayed him.
Matthew 10:1-4

For further understanding of your talents, examine these five insights and select those that describe you best.

☐ You see each person as a distinct, one-of-a-kind individual.

☐ You can see how people who are very different can work together.

☐ You can build productive teams of people because you can see the talents of people and then structure groups around those talents.

☐ Because you see individuals so distinctly and try to relate to them in terms of their specific characteristics, relating to people can be taxing and even overwhelming.

☐ Individualization talents are valuable because they help you form powerful relationships with people. Those people know that you take them seriously and that you see them as distinct individuals. For many, this is very valuable, as it brings trust and intensity to your relationships.

INPUT

You are inquisitive. You collect things. You might collect information — words, facts, books, and quotations — or you might collect tangible objects such as butterflies, baseball cards, porcelain dolls, or sepia photographs. Whatever you collect, you collect it because it interests you. And yours is the kind of mind that finds so many things interesting. The world is exciting precisely because of its infinite variety and complexity. If you read a great deal, it is not necessarily to refine your theories but, rather, to add more information to your archives. If you like to travel, it is because each new location offers novel artifacts and facts. These can be acquired and then stored away. Why are they worth storing? At the time of storing it is often hard to say exactly when or why you might need them, but who knows when they might become useful? With all those possible uses in mind, you really don't feel comfortable throwing anything away. So you keep acquiring and compiling and filing stuff away. It's interesting. It keeps your mind fresh. And perhaps one day some of it will prove valuable.

Scriptures that relate to the Input theme:

There are also many other things that Jesus did, but if these were to be described individually, I do not think the whole world would contain the books that would be written.
John 21:25

When you come, bring the cloak I left with Carpus in Troas, the papyrus rolls, and especially the parchments.
2 Timothy 4:13

My son, if you receive my words
and treasure my commands,
Turning your ear to wisdom,
inclining your heart to understanding;
Yes, if you call to intelligence,
and to understanding raise your voice;
If you seek her like silver,
and like hidden treasures search her out:

Then will you understand the fear of the LORD;
the knowledge of God you will find;
For the LORD gives wisdom,
from his mouth come knowledge and understanding;
Proverbs 2:1-6

For further understanding of your talents, examine these five insights and select those that describe you best.

☐ You always want to know more. You crave information.

☐ You like to collect certain things, such as ideas, books, memorabilia, quotations, and facts.

☐ You have an active curiosity. You find many things very interesting.

☐ You may have difficulty getting started or completing a project because you feel like you never have enough information. Going to a library or "surfing the Net" may turn into hours once your curiosity takes off, and you may have difficulties filing and housing all of the information and ideas you acquire.

☐ Input talents are valuable because they keep your mind active and lead you to become knowledgeable. You are likely to become an expert in one or more areas.

INTELLECTION

You like to think. You like mental activity. You like exercising the "muscles" of your brain, stretching them in multiple directions. This need for mental activity may be focused; for example, you may be trying to solve a problem or develop an idea or understand another person's feelings. The exact focus will depend on your other strengths. On the other hand, this mental activity may very well lack focus. The theme of Intellection does not dictate what you are thinking about; it simply describes that you like to think. You are the kind of person who enjoys your time alone because it is your time for musing and reflection. You are introspective. In a sense you are your own best companion, as you pose yourself questions and try out answers on yourself to see how they sound. This introspection may lead you to a slight sense of discontent as you compare what you are actually doing with all the thoughts and ideas that your mind conceives. Or this introspection may tend toward more pragmatic matters such as the events of the day or a conversation that you plan to have later. Wherever it leads you, this mental hum is one of the constants of your life.

Scriptures that relate to the Intellection theme:

After three days they found him in the temple, sitting in the midst of the teachers, listening to them and asking them questions, and all who heard him were astounded at his understanding and his answers.
Luke 2:46-47

So he debated in the synagogue with the Jews and with the worshipers, and daily in the public square with whoever happened to be there. Even some of the Epicurean and Stoic philosophers engaged him in discussion. Some asked, "What is this scavenger trying to say?" Others said, "He sounds like

a promoter of foreign deities," because he was preaching about 'Jesus' and 'Resurrection.'"
Acts 17:17-18

He said to him, "You shall love the Lord, your God, with all your heart, with all your soul, and with all your mind."
Matthew 22:37

Therefore, gird up the loins of your mind, live soberly, and set your hopes completely on the grace to be brought to you at the revelation of Jesus Christ.
1 Peter 1:13

For further understanding of your talents, examine these five insights and select those that describe you best.

☐ You love to study, and you prefer intellectual discussions.

☐ You like to think and to let your thoughts go in many directions.

☐ You like to spend time alone so you can reflect and ponder.

☐ You may become discouraged because there are so many things that you need to think about so carefully and thoroughly.

☐ Intellection talents are valuable because they help you find innovative ideas and solutions.

LEARNER

You love to learn. The subject matter that interests you most will be determined by your other themes and experiences, but whatever the subject, you will always be drawn to the process of learning. The process, more than the content or the result, is especially exciting for you. You are energized by the steady and deliberate journey from ignorance to competence. The thrill of the first few facts, the early efforts to recite or practice what you have learned, the growing confidence of a skill mastered — this is the process that entices you. Your excitement leads you to engage in adult learning experiences — yoga or piano lessons or graduate classes. It enables you to thrive in dynamic work environments where you are asked to take on short project assignments and are expected to learn a lot about the new subject matter in a short period of time and then move on to the next one. This Learner theme does not necessarily mean that you seek to become the subject matter expert, or that you are striving for the respect that accompanies a professional or academic credential. The outcome of the learning is less significant than the "getting there."

Scriptures that relate to the Learner theme:

The king told Ashpenaz, his chief chamberlain, to bring in some of the Israelites of royal blood and of the nobility, young men without any defect, handsome, intelligent and wise, quick to learn, and prudent in judgment, such as could take their place in the king's palace; they were to be taught the language and literature of the Chaldeans...
Daniel 1:3-4

As they continued their journey he entered a village where a woman whose name was Martha welcomed him. She had a sister named Mary (who) sat beside the Lord at his feet listening to him speak. Martha, burdened with

much serving, came to him and said, "Lord, do you not care that my sister has left me by myself to do the serving? Tell her to help me." The Lord said to her in reply, "Martha, Martha, you are anxious and worried about many things. There is need of only one thing. Mary has chosen the better part and it will not be taken from her."
Luke 10:38-42

Ezra had set his heart on the study and practice of the law of the LORD and on teaching statutes and ordinances in Israel.
Ezra 7:10

But you, remain faithful to what you have learned and believed, because you know from whom you learned it, and that from infancy you have known (the) sacred scriptures, which are capable of giving you wisdom for salvation through faith in Christ Jesus. All scripture is inspired by God and is useful for teaching, for refutation, for correction, and for training in righteousness, so that one who belongs to God may be competent, equipped for every good work.
2 Timothy 3:14-17

For further understanding of your talents, examine these five insights and select those that describe you best.

☐ You want to continuously learn and improve.

☐ You enjoy the process of learning as much as what you actually learn.

☐ You get a thrill out of learning new facts, beginning a new subject, and mastering an important skill. Learning builds your confidence.

☐ You can get frustrated about wanting to learn so many different things because you fear you'll never be an expert.

☐ Learner talents are valuable because they propel you to thrive in a dynamic world where learning is a necessity. You can learn a lot in a short period of time.

MAXIMIZER

Excellence, not average, is your measure. Taking something from below average to slightly above average takes a great deal of effort and in your opinion is not very rewarding. Transforming something strong into something superb takes just as much effort but is much more thrilling. Strengths, whether yours or someone else's, fascinate you. Like a diver after pearls, you search them out, watching for the telltale signs of a strength. A glimpse of untutored excellence, rapid learning, a skill mastered without recourse to steps — all these are clues that a strength may be in play. And having found a strength, you feel compelled to nurture it, refine it, and stretch it toward excellence. You polish the pearl until it shines. This natural sorting of strengths means that others see you as discriminating. You choose to spend time with people who appreciate your particular strengths. Likewise, you are attracted to others who seem to have found and cultivated their own strengths. You tend to avoid those who want to fix you and make you well-rounded. You don't want to spend your life bemoaning what you lack. Rather, you want to capitalize on the gifts with which you are blessed. It's more fun. It's more productive. And, counterintuitively, it is more demanding.

Scriptures that relate to the Maximizer theme:

Now as you excel in every respect, in faith, discourse, knowledge, all earnestness, and in the love we have for you, may you excel in this gracious act also.
2 Corinthians 8:7

From all the gifts that you receive, and from the best parts, you are to consecrate to the Lord your own full contribution.
Numbers 18:29

They that hope in the LORD *will renew their strength,*
they will soar as with eagles' wings;
They will run and not grow weary,
walk and not grow faint.
Isaiah 40:31

After a long time the master of those servants came back and settled accounts
with them. The one who had received five talents came forward bringing
the additional five. He said, "Master, you gave me five talents. See, I have
made five more." His master said to him, "Well done, my good and faithful
servant. Since you were faithful in small matters, I will give you great
responsibilities. Come, share your master's joy."
Matthew 25:19-21

For this reason, I remind you to stir into flame the gift of God that you have
through the imposition of my hands.
2 Timothy 1:6

For further understanding of your talents, examine these five insights and select those that describe you best.

☐ You see talents and strengths in others, sometimes before they do.

☐ You love to help others become excited by the potential of their natural talents.

☐ You have the capacity to see what people will do best and which jobs they will be good at. You can see how people's talents match the tasks that must be completed.

☐ Some people will be intimidated by your perceptiveness and drive for excellence. These people may want to keep you at a distance, and you may feel rejected or like there is something wrong with you.

☐ Maximizer talents are valuable because they help you focus on talents to stimulate personal and group excellence. If a group or organization is on the move toward excellence, a talented Maximizer is probably somewhere in the midst.

POSITIVITY

You are generous with praise, quick to smile, and always on the lookout for the positive in the situation. Some call you lighthearted. Others just wish that their glass were as full as yours seems to be. But either way, people want to be around you. Their world looks better around you because your enthusiasm is contagious. Lacking your energy and optimism, some find their world drab with repetition or, worse, heavy with pressure. You seem to find a way to lighten their spirit. You inject drama into every project. You celebrate every achievement. You find ways to make everything more exciting and more vital. Some cynics may reject your energy, but you are rarely dragged down. Your Positivity won't allow it. Somehow you can't quite escape your conviction that it is good to be alive, that work can be fun, and that no matter what the setbacks, one must never lose one's sense of humor.

Scriptures that relate to the Positivity theme:

A joyful heart is the health of the body,
but a depressed spirit dries up the bones.
Proverbs 17:22

Finally, brothers, whatever is true, whatever is honorable, whatever is just,
whatever is pure, whatever is lovely, whatever is gracious, if there is any ex-
cellence and if there is anything worthy of praise, think about these things.
Philippians 4:8

Rejoice always. Pray without ceasing. In all circumstances give thanks, for
this is the will of God for you in Christ Jesus.
1 Thessalonians 5:16-18

He said further: "Go, eat rich foods and drink sweet drinks, and allot portions to those who had nothing prepared; for today is holy to our LORD. Do not be saddened this day, for rejoicing in the LORD must be your strength!"
Nehemiah 8:10

But now we must celebrate and rejoice, because your brother was dead and has come to life again; he was lost and has been found.
Luke 15:32

For further understanding of your talents, examine these five insights and select those that describe you best.

☐ You bring enthusiasm to people, groups, and organizations.

☐ You can stimulate people to be more productive and become more hopeful.

☐ You can get people excited about what they are doing, and therefore they become more productive.

☐ Some people will criticize you for being so optimistic. They may say you are naïve, and that may cause you to doubt yourself.

☐ Positivity talents are valuable because they have such a helpful influence on the attitudes, motivation, and productive behaviors of others. Groups and individuals are energized to move toward excellence.

RELATOR

Relator describes your attitude toward your relationships. In simple terms, the Relator theme pulls you toward people you already know. You do not necessarily shy away from meeting new people — in fact, you may have other themes that cause you to enjoy the thrill of turning strangers into friends — but you do derive a great deal of pleasure and strength from being around your close friends. You are comfortable with intimacy. Once the initial connection has been made, you deliberately encourage a deepening of the relationship. You want to understand their feelings, their goals, their fears, and their dreams; and you want them to understand yours. You know that this kind of closeness implies a certain amount of risk — you might be taken advantage of — but you are willing to accept that risk. For you a relationship has value only if it is genuine. And the only way to know that is to entrust yourself to the other person. The more you share with each other, the more you risk together. The more you risk together, the more each of you proves your caring is genuine. These are your steps toward real friendship, and you take them willingly.

Scriptures that relate to the Relator theme:

Some friends bring ruin on us,
but a true friend is more loyal than a brother.
Proverbs 18:24

Two are better than one: they get a good wage for their labor. If the one falls, the other will lift up his companion. Woe to the solitary man! For if he should fall, he has no one to lift him up. So also, if two sleep together, they keep each other warm. How can one alone keep warm? Where a lone man may be overcome, two together can resist. A three-ply cord is not easily broken.

Ecclesiastes 4:9-12

Saul discussed his intention of killing David with his son Jonathan and with all his servants. But Saul's son Jonathan, who was very fond of David, told him: "My father Saul is trying to kill you. Therefore, please be on your guard tomorrow morning; get out of sight and remain in hiding. I, however, will go out and stand beside my father in the countryside where you are, and will speak to him about you. If I learn anything, I will let you know." [...the name of Jonathan must never be allowed by the family of David to die out from among you, or the LORD will make you answer for it." And in his love for David, Jonathan renewed his oath to him, because he loved him as his very self.]

1 Samuel 19:1-3, 20:16-17

For further understanding of your talents, examine these five insights and select those that describe you best.

☐ You can form close relationships with people, and you enjoy doing so.

☐ You receive profound satisfaction from working hard with friends to accomplish an important goal.

☐ You know many people, and you can relate with all kinds of people. But you also have a very small group of friends with whom you have an incredibly deep relationship.

☐ Some people may feel threatened or uncomfortable because they can't bring themselves to have the close, intense personal relationships that you thrive on.

☐ Relator talents are valuable to organizations, groups, and individuals because they foster interpersonal relationships that lead to productivity.

RESPONSIBILITY

Your Responsibility theme forces you to take psychological ownership for anything you commit to, and whether large or small, you feel emotionally bound to follow it through to completion. Your good name depends on it. If for some reason you cannot deliver, you automatically start to look for ways to make it up to the other person. Apologies are not enough. Excuses and rationalizations are totally unacceptable. You will not quite be able to live with yourself until you have made restitution. This conscientiousness, this near obsession for doing things right, and your impeccable ethics combine to create your reputation: utterly dependable. When assigning new responsibilities, people will look to you first because they know things will get done. When people come to you for help — and they soon will — you must be selective. Your willingness to volunteer may sometimes lead you to take on more than you should.

Scriptures that relate to the Responsibility theme:

Therefore the supervisors and satraps tried to find grounds for accusation against Daniel as regards the administration. But they could accuse him of no wrongdoing; because he was trustworthy, no fault of neglect or misconduct was to be found in him.
Daniel 6:5

A good name is more desirable than great riches,
*   and high esteem, than gold and silver.*
Proverbs 22:1

"Not everyone who says to me, 'Lord, Lord,' will enter the kingdom of heaven, but only the one who does the will of my Father in heaven."
Matthew 7:21

"Then the king will say to those on his right, 'Come, you who are blessed by my Father. Inherit the kingdom prepared for you from the foundation of the world. For I was hungry and you gave me food, I was thirsty and you gave me drink, a stranger and you welcomed me, naked and you clothed me, ill and you cared for me, in prison and you visited me.' Then the righteous will answer him and say, 'Lord, when did we see you hungry and feed you, or thirsty and give you drink? When did we see you a stranger and welcome you, or naked and clothe you? When did we see you ill or in prison, and visit you?' And the king will say to them in reply, 'Amen, I say to you, whatever you did for one of these least brothers of mine, you did for me.'"
Matthew 25:34-40

For further understanding of your talents, examine these five insights and select those that describe you best.

- ☐ You are dependable, and people know they can count on you.

- ☐ You don't want to let people down, and you will work very hard to fulfill all your responsibilities and keep your word.

- ☐ You have many obligations and commitments because so many people know that they can count on you. Therefore, more and more people come to you.

- ☐ With the responsibility you feel to the people who come to you and with the demands that each of them brings, you often feel overwhelmed and under pressure to perform.

- ☐ Responsibility talents are valuable because they lead others to trust you and to become more responsible themselves. You might be more of a role model than you realize.

RESTORATIVE

You love to solve problems. Whereas some are dismayed when they encounter yet another breakdown, you can be energized by it. You enjoy the challenge of analyzing the symptoms, identifying what is wrong, and finding the solution. You may prefer practical problems or conceptual ones or personal ones. You may seek out specific kinds of problems that you have met many times before and that you are confident you can fix. Or you may feel the greatest push when faced with complex and unfamiliar problems. Your exact preferences are determined by your other themes and experiences. But what is certain is that you enjoy bringing things back to life. It is a wonderful feeling to identify the undermining factor(s), eradicate them, and restore something to its true glory. Intuitively, you know that without your intervention, this thing — this machine, this technique, this person, this company — might have ceased to function. You fixed it, resuscitated it, rekindled its vitality. Phrasing it the way you might, you saved it.

Scriptures that relate to the Restorative theme:

Then Levi gave a great banquet for him in his house, and a large crowd of tax collectors and others were at table with them. The Pharisees and their scribes complained to his disciples, saying, "Why do you eat and drink with tax collectors and sinners?" Jesus said to them in reply, "Those who are healthy do not need a physician, but the sick do. I have not come to call the righteous to repentance but sinners."
Luke 5:29-32

Brothers, even if a person is caught in some transgression, you who are spiritual should correct that one in a gentle spirit, looking to yourself, so that you also may not be tempted.
Galatians 6:1

The LORD *is my shepherd;*
  there is nothing I lack.
In green pastures you let me graze;
  to safe waters you lead me;
  you restore my strength.
Psalm 23:1-3

For further understanding of your talents, examine these five insights and select those that describe you best.

☐ You readily take on projects that others believe "can't be saved."

☐ You can analyze a situation and identify potential shortcomings and what needs to be fixed.

☐ You quickly recognize problems that others may not detect.

☐ Other people may not like the fact that you can so quickly determine the problems and weaknesses in people, situations, and organizations. They may find this ability embarrassing, even if your assessments and solutions are accurate.

☐ Restorative talents are valuable because through them you are energized, rather than defeated, by problems.

SELF-ASSURANCE

Self-Assurance is similar to self-confidence. In the deepest part of you, you have faith in your strengths. You know that you are able — able to take risks, able to meet new challenges, able to stake claims, and, most important, able to deliver. But Self-Assurance is more than just self-confidence. Blessed with the theme of Self-Assurance, you have confidence not only in your abilities but in your judgment. When you look at the world, you know that your perspective is unique and distinct. And because no one sees exactly what you see, you know that no one can make your decisions for you. No one can tell you what to think. They can guide. They can suggest. But you alone have the authority to form conclusions, make decisions, and act. This authority, this final accountability for the living of your life, does not intimidate you. On the contrary, it feels natural to you. No matter what the situation, you seem to know what the right decision is. This theme lends you an aura of certainty. Unlike many, you are not easily swayed by someone else's arguments, no matter how persuasive they may be. This Self-Assurance may be quiet or loud, depending on your other themes, but it is solid. It is strong. Like the keel of a ship, it withstands many different pressures and keeps you on your course.

Scriptures that relate to the Self-Assurance theme:

Faith is the realization of what is hoped for and evidence of things not seen.
Hebrews 11:1

On this account I am suffering these things; but I am not ashamed, for I know him in whom I have believed and am confident that he is able to guard what has been entrusted to me until that day.
2 Timothy 1:12

135

Then he had another dream, and this one, too, he told to his brothers. "I had another dream," he said; "this time, the sun and the moon and eleven stars were bowing down to me." When he also told it to his father, his father reproved him. "What is the meaning of this dream of yours?" he asked. "Can it be that I and your mother and your brothers are to come and bow to the ground before you?" So his brothers were wrought up against him but his father pondered the matter.
Genesis 37:9-11

For further understanding of your talents, examine these five insights and select those that describe you best.

☐ You are confident about your ability to manage your life.

☐ You can "bounce back" from disappointments and crises.

☐ You believe that your decisions are right and that your perspective is unique and distinct.

☐ Other people may see your self-assurance as a type of pride or arrogance. Some people may criticize you when they wish that they had your confidence. Sometimes people want to get close to you because they hope that some of your confidence will rub off on them. But other people will keep you away because they don't have your confidence and are afraid that you will see through them.

☐ Self-Assurance talents are valuable because they keep you strong as you withstand many pressures, as you stay on your course, and as you willingly claim the authority to form conclusions, make decisions, and act.

SIGNIFICANCE

You want to be very significant in the eyes of other people. In the truest sense of the word you want to be recognized. You want to be heard. You want to stand out. You want to be known. In particular, you want to be known and appreciated for the unique strengths you bring. You feel a need to be admired as credible, professional, and successful. Likewise, you want to associate with others who are credible, professional, and successful. And if they aren't, you will push them to achieve until they are. Or you will move on. An independent spirit, you want your work to be a way of life rather than a job, and in that work you want to be given free rein, the leeway to do things your way. Your yearnings feel intense to you, and you honor those yearnings. And so your life is filled with goals, achievements, or qualifications that you crave. Whatever your focus — and each person is distinct — your Significance theme will keep pulling you upward, away from the mediocre toward the exceptional. It is the theme that keeps you reaching.

Scriptures that relate to the Significance theme:

You are the light of the world. A city set on a mountain cannot be hidden. Nor do they light a lamp and then put it under a bushel basket; it is set on a lampstand, where it gives light to all in the house. Just so, your light must shine before others, that they may see your good deeds and glorify your heavenly Father.
Matthew 5:14-16

"...I came so that they might have life and have it more abundantly."
John 10:10

Even if you should have countless guides to Christ, yet you do not have many fathers, for I became your father in Christ Jesus through the gospel. Therefore, I urge you, be imitators of me.
1 Corinthians 4:15-16

For further understanding of your talents, examine these five insights and select those that describe you best.

☐ You probably enjoy receiving public recognition for the differences you make.

☐ You want to have an impact on other people, groups, and society as a whole.

☐ You want the contributions you make to be viewed as substantial, powerful, and significant.

☐ Although many people will appreciate your talent in this theme, others may be intimidated by it, and they might not say so. Instead, they may say that you are "just wanting attention" or that you are egocentric.

☐ Significance talents are valuable because they can be a source of energy for doing good and helpful things that will outlive you. You are motivated by a driving force to produce transformational, lasting change.

STRATEGIC

The Strategic theme enables you to sort through the clutter and find the best route. It is not a skill that can be taught. It is a distinct way of thinking, a special perspective on the world at large. This perspective allows you to see patterns where others simply see complexity. Mindful of these patterns, you play out alternative scenarios, always asking, "What if this happened? Okay, well what if this happened?" This recurring question helps you see around the next corner. There you can evaluate accurately the potential obstacles. Guided by where you see each path leading, you start to make selections. You discard the paths that lead nowhere. You discard the paths that lead straight into resistance. You discard the paths that lead into a fog of confusion. You cull and make selections until you arrive at the chosen path — your strategy. Armed with your strategy, you strike forward. This is your Strategic theme at work: "What if?" Select. Strike.

Scriptures that relate to the Strategic theme:

Many gathered together so that there was no longer room for them, not even around the door, and he preached the word to them. They came bringing to him a paralytic carried by four men. Unable to get near Jesus because of the crowd, they opened up the roof above him. After they had broken through, they let down the mat on which the paralytic was lying.
Mark 2:2-4

Make known to me your ways, Lord;
teach me your paths.
Guide me in your truth and teach me,
for you are God my savior.
For you I wait all the long day,
because of your goodness, Lord.
Psalm 25:4-5

139

Without knowledge even zeal is not good;
  and he who acts hastily, blunders.
Proverbs 19:2

No trial has come to you but what is human. God is faithful and will not let you be tried beyond your strength; but with the trial he will also provide a way out, so that you may be able to bear it.
1 Corinthians 10:13

For further understanding of your talents, examine these five insights and select those that describe you best.

☐ You create multiple ways to do things.

☐ You can quickly pick out the relevant issues and patterns when confronted by problems and complexities.

☐ You have a "What if this happens?" mentality toward work and life. This type of questioning helps you see, plan, and prepare for future situations.

☐ Some may criticize you for not moving on issues as quickly as they may like, but you know that there is great wisdom in reviewing all of the potential problems and searching for the alternative that will work best.

☐ Strategic talents are valuable because they enable you to quickly reach goals by seeing the pros and cons of various alternatives. You carefully consider the whole picture and then generate the most effective set of actions or routes to take.

WOO

Woo stands for winning others over. You enjoy the challenge of meeting new people and getting them to like you. Strangers are rarely intimidating to you. On the contrary, strangers can be energizing. You are drawn to them. You want to learn their names, ask them questions, and find some area of common interest so that you can strike up a conversation and build rapport. Some people shy away from starting up conversations because they worry about running out of things to say. You don't. Not only are you rarely at a loss for words, you actually enjoy initiating with strangers because you derive satisfaction from breaking the ice and making a connection. Once that connection is made, you are quite happy to wrap it up and move on. There are new people to meet, new rooms to work, new crowds to mingle in. In your world there are no strangers, only friends you haven't met yet — lots of them.

Scriptures that relate to the Woo theme:

Do not neglect hospitality, for through it some have unknowingly entertained angels.
Hebrews 13:2

At the sight of the crowds, his heart was moved with pity for them because they were troubled and abandoned, like sheep without a shepherd. Then he said to his disciples, "The harvest is abundant but the laborers are few; so ask the master of the harvest to send out laborers for his harvest."
Matthew 9:36-38

Conduct yourselves wisely toward outsiders, making the most of the opportunity.
Colossians 4:5

For further understanding of your talents, examine these five insights and select those that describe you best.

☐ You have the capacity to quickly connect with people and generate positive responses from them.

☐ You can enter a crowd of people and easily know what to do and what to say.

☐ You see no strangers, only friends you haven't met yet.

☐ Because you know so many people, some may believe that you form only shallow relationships. Others, however, will envy the way you make friends.

☐ Woo talents are valuable because people are influenced by your ability to draw them into a group or relationship.

STRENGTHS STORIES

Amid Adversity, He Found Confidence

A gentleman named Henry came in for coaching because his job was being phased out and he didn't know what to do. He was responsible for his family, and he was understandably upset. He didn't want to let anyone down, but his industry was shrinking, and he was in a real bind.

At his coaching sessions, he simply thought about his five Signature Themes and how they impact his world. He learned that his Relator talents made him more effective in long-term customer relationships than in quick transactions. Because of his Responsibility talents, he's "straight up" with his customers. He doesn't blindside them with the fine print.

As the coaching process moved along, he began to see his Signature Themes as the solid foundation on which he operates. What's more, as he learned more about his greatest talents, he became more and more confident. That increased self-assurance led him to take confident actions, and he is now a successful business owner in a different field. And as you would expect, his customers find him reliable, honest, and connected to their needs.

Kristy McAdams
Lutz, Florida, United States

All in the Family

Eighteen months ago, each member of our family learned our Signature Themes. This included my wife and me, our three children, our two daughters-in-law, and even our daughter's boyfriend. The ensuing conversations dominated our weekly family dinner for many months.

We first discussed each person's top five themes and possible applications of talents from those themes. That took about three months. We then had follow-up discussions about how that was going and what else we could do to build on our talents. I completed the Strengths Performance Coaching course in mid-2007, and I am now working through a coaching process with each family member.

We have observed the greatest talents of each member being applied in various strengths since we first learned our top five themes. Those activities range from arranging Christmas dinner to the roles each of us play in our local church. We also have applied what we've learned about our talents to employment situations. When we discuss job-change opportunities or confronting other situations, our Signature Themes are now an important part of the conversation.

Overall, our level of communication has improved a great deal. The powerful presence of Empathy talents in my wife, my daughter, one of my sons, and his wife is a great asset now that we better understand them. The rest of us didn't quite get what was going on before! There is also a lot of Input talent in our family, so there are plenty of book discussions, and there is a high level of interest in understanding more about talents and strengths. In fact, several members of our family are lining up to qualify as coaches this year.

Rob Nicholls
Box Hill South, Victoria, Australia

Expressing God's Purpose

During my college years, I was (like most other college students) searching for my place in this world. As life whirled around me, I craved a better understanding of myself. That's when the whole strengths concept entered the picture, and I learned my Signature Themes. I didn't want to be put in a box, and I didn't want to place parameters around others in my world, but I found it refreshing that through my top five I could articulate some of my personality and tendencies.

In a quest to filter my talents through my Christian worldview, I learned that the way in which I am "wired" is Designed. I have appreciated the message that my tendencies are not merely parts of my personality; they are talents that give me potential for strength in many areas. Knowing that my Signature Themes and the talents they offer are by Design has helped me in conversations with my peers, my staff, and my supervisor: I now have descriptions about what makes me feel strong and how I can best use those talents for God's Kingdom.

God created us for His purposes, so it seems wonderful that I feel strong for His good work — and now I can purposefully find ways to express myself through my talents and fulfill my God-given potential.

Kristine Wendt
Lino Lakes/White Bear Lake/Spring Lake Park
Minnesota, United States

Transformed by Self-Awareness

Mark had been appointed interim youth director just before I accepted the assignment of interim pastor of a great Southern California university church. Upon assuming the role and assessing the staff, I found Mark to be very excited about his ministry to youth. He tackled his assignment with great gusto and enthusiasm.

Mark had just returned from the eastern part of the United States, where he had tried a stint as a sportswriter. He was very passionate about that vocation, but it was slow going for his wife and him financially, so they came back home to regroup and find some direction. He had a college degree but nowhere to go. He lived with a high level of frustration.

Soon after I arrived, I had each staff member take the StrengthsFinder assessment. The connection with Mark was immediate — an AHA! moment, for sure. He wanted to talk about talent discovery and strengths development at every opportunity. He studied, read, and conversed about strengths with everyone who would take a moment. A revolution was taking place right before our eyes.

Mark worked very hard as a youth director, but, as time went by, I noted that some of the early gusto and enthusiasm was beginning to wane. Youth ministry was not his life's passion. As he studied and began to own his greatest talents, his self-awareness was growing, and he began to realize that he was a talented writer who would be excited about teaching at the university level. A university had spotted his ability, and his major professor, who knew of Mark's talents, opened the door for a future in teaching and writing.

Mark had found himself, and he had then found his direction. He enrolled in a major university and will soon graduate with his Ph.D. He will teach and write with passion, because that is where his potential for true strength lies, and it is who he is.

Mark has never looked back, and he has an absolutely brilliant future ahead of him. He was transformed by self-awareness and an opportunity to make informed decisions from the inside out.

Clari Kinzler
San Diego, California, United States

Growing Without Guilt

Strengths training changed the way I look at myself and my work. I took a class and some personal coaching in the area of talent discovery and strengths development.

To tell the truth, I wasn't all that excited by the prospect of another "personality test." But StrengthsFinder was significantly different. It was absolutely liberating. The strengths training gave me permission to have lots of fun in the areas that I enjoyed and was good at, and it gave me an absolute reason not to work in areas that were outside of my greatest talents. It meant that I could grow without guilt. It meant that I could say no with solid reasons, rather than lame excuses. And the class was transformational: Each of us in the class grew in exciting and amazing ways.

Our newfound knowledge changed how we related and communicated with one another. I even used information about my talents and strengths in my application for admission to seminary.

As I tell others, "Stop dwelling on your weaknesses, and get going with your strengths!"

Judy Green-Davis
Phoenix, Arizona, United States

CHAPTER 5

Using Your Talents for Growth and Service

You've learned about the talents associated with each of your five Signature Themes. Are you wondering how to apply these talents in your parish and in your life? Actually, they already play a part in the choices you make every day. It just happens naturally.

Consider Bob, Kathy, Donna, and Ray, who all went on a two-week trip to the Holy Land with a group from their parish. Bob has Context as a Signature Theme, so it's not surprising that the first thing he did in preparation for the journey was study the history of the region. He wanted to understand the roots of the current situation in Jerusalem.

One of Kathy's Signature Themes is Woo, so one of her goals for the trip was to befriend everyone else who was going. In her world, there are no strangers, only new friends yet to be met. She expected to come home from this trip with 25 new pals.

Donna's Signature Themes include Discipline, so she wanted a detailed itinerary. She had to know what to pack and what to expect each day.

Ray, on the other hand, has Adaptability as one of his Signature Themes. He wasn't at all bothered by the fact that the travel plans weren't finalized until three days before they left. And he didn't mind that the daily schedule got altered on the fly. In fact, he greeted the exciting changes that each new day brought.

Your greatest talents don't come into play only during life's big events — you use them every day. Do you set out your clothes the night before, or do you decide what to wear just before you get dressed in the morning? Do you try something new on the menu when you go to a restaurant, or do you simply order the same thing most of the time? Do you make quick decisions about what movie to see or book to read, or do you ponder and weigh options first? Do you talk to the people in line with you at the grocery store, or do you flip through a magazine? Your talents filter the way you approach every single situation you encounter and every decision you make.

Your talents also influence how you grow spiritually and the ways you serve God and others through your parish. If the parish ministry coordinator had taken the time to help Rick, the disgruntled greeter from Chapter 1, identify his talents and assume a role that built on those talents, Rick's parish would have gained a more loyal, spiritually productive member.

Knowing your talents when you join a new parish can help you avoid the pitfalls of serving in a role that doesn't quite fit. When you know your talents, you naturally try to find ways to live them out.

Phil understands this. When he was growing up, his family belonged to a very strict Protestant church. "You couldn't dance, you couldn't listen to rock and roll music, you couldn't go to the skating rink because they played rock and roll music, you couldn't go to the bowling alley because they drank there, you couldn't go shoot pool," he recalls. "There were so many things you couldn't do, and so I grew up left out of a lot of things. Kids would have parties, and of course I couldn't go." Those experiences weighed heavily on Phil, and he became "de-churched" for a while as a young adult. But when he got married, he converted to Catholicism — primarily because his new wife's parish made him feel wanted.

Includer is Phil's top theme, so he reaches out to everyone — he doesn't want anyone to feel left out like he did growing up. Phil's personal mission is "to look for the wallflowers, or the old people who are sitting by themselves, or the handicapped, or those who are not included — and include them."

Phil says he tries "to show love across the board to all people," and his upbringing had a big part in that. "But," he continues, "my desire to reach out to practically everyone is obviously a natural part of me. I just love people."

Your talents also influence the way you approach your growth and study. This is especially true in your study of the Scriptures. One of Sarah's Signature Themes is Individualization, and that influences how her faith has grown. "I think the way I studied the Bible and learned from it was through its characters," she says. She appreciates the uniqueness of those characters and seeks inspiration from them. "I love the story of Esther; I love the story of Joseph; I love the story of Paul." But her favorite Bible character is Esther. "I love the whole story, how she was a nothing and became the queen. With great courage, this woman of nothingness went before the king to save her people, even though she didn't want to do it. But she did. She drew her belief from the bottom of her being, and with the support of others, through prayer and fasting, and asking God to make a way for her, she went. So when I am facing a difficult task, I think of Esther, and she becomes my courage."

FOCUS ON OUTCOMES

Phil and Sarah are effectively putting their talents to work in their spiritual lives. They know how to find fulfillment. You might be tempted to imitate them. But beware: One of the most common mistakes people make in their spiritual lives is to focus on the *steps to spiritual growth* rather than on the *outcomes of spiritual growth*. Often, people will look at the lives of spiritually mature individuals and try to replicate the steps these individuals took to achieve maturity in their own lives.

The mistake is assuming that if two people follow the same steps, pattern, or procedures, they will produce the same outcomes in their lives. This goes against everything that Gallup's talent research reveals. You may want to achieve the outcome of spiritual maturity, but the steps you take to successfully achieve that goal will depend greatly on your unique talents.

Let us illustrate. One of the goals for all the members of Brian's parish is for their faith to be involved in every aspect of their lives. Intellection is one of Brian's Signature Themes, so he has to think about things — a lot. He needs to take time to ponder and ruminate on concepts, and not only that, he is constantly thinking about all manner of topics. "The best way for me to reach this goal," Brian says, "and I think it's an important goal for all Christians, is to start each day by reading the Bible and also some thought-provoking, challenging books about spiritual concepts. Then I can think about what I've read throughout the day, and I think to myself, 'How does what I studied this morning relate to what I'm doing right now?' This really helps me pay attention and think about my faith more deeply."

Shauna is a member of the same parish, and she takes a different approach. "I found out that I have Activator as one of my Signature Themes, and that really explained a lot to me. I always thought our parish's Lenten

Bible studies where you just sit around and read the Bible and just talk about it were really, really boring," she says.

Shauna used to feel guilty about this, until she learned that Activators can get bored easily. They have to *do* something for their faith to grow, not just *talk* about something. "So I got involved in delivering meals to the elderly and homebound, and because I'm actually doing something for someone and I can see the results, I've found that I'm really starting to grow in my faith. I just need to be involved in doing something meaningful, and I find that involvement spills out into every other area of my life." Now, instead of feeling guilty about her talents, she feels good about the way her talents help her make a difference in the lives of others.

Both Brian and Shauna are achieving their goal — making faith central to every aspect of their lives — but they are doing it in very different ways. The outcome is the same for both, but the steps they take to reach the outcome are different — because they have different talents.

USING TALENTS TO FORGIVE

Your talents determine how you approach solving problems in your spiritual life. Take the doctrine of forgiveness. How you forgive others depends a great deal on your talents. "I've always been the type of person who gets my feelings hurt easily," recalls Melissa. Because of that, she has always found it hard to forgive people who have hurt her deeply. "I used to feel like a failure as a Christian, because we're supposed to forgive, right? Because God forgave us in Jesus' death and resurrection, we're supposed to forgive others. When I found out that I had a lot of talent in Empathy, it all made sense — I could so strongly feel others' emotions toward me in those hurtful situations, and because of my empathy, it was hard to let go of those feelings."

But then Melissa figured out a way to help her forgive and get past the hurt. "Usually, when people find out they've hurt me," she says, "they're sorry about it and feel pretty bad about it. So instead of focusing on my feelings about it, I focus on theirs. I imagine what they must feel like. I put myself in their shoes and know how bad I would feel if I hurt someone I cared about. Putting myself in their position and feeling their feelings helps me get past my own hurt and move on to forgiveness."

Craig, on the other hand, has always been quick to forgive others. His Harmony talents certainly are the key. "I just want people to get along," he says, "and I want to get along with everybody too. But I'm not a doormat either — I also have a lot of Command. I know that seems like a weird combination, but it's how I approach the world." When he feels wronged or hurt by someone, Craig can confront the situation or the person fairly quickly. Not one to hold a grudge, he can forgive quickly too. "I want to resolve the issue so that we can get the relationship back on track," he says. "Letting things fester only makes matters worse and makes it harder for people to get along with each other. Forgiveness helps restore the peace."

Forgiveness is a central doctrine and expectation of the Christian faith. But the way Christians forgive — the steps to the outcome — depends on their unique combination of talents. To grow spiritually and live the life God intends you to live, you need to focus on the outcomes you want to achieve and let your talents determine the best way to get there.

Your talents are a precious gift from God. They influence how you see, experience, and make your contribution to the world. The following pages list insights, thought-provoking questions, and action suggestions that can help you build on your talents to create and apply strengths — and to grow spiritually and serve God and others in the process. Choose those that you feel best match your talents and values, and put them to use as you develop your personal plan for growth and service.

ACHIEVER

If you are particularly talented in Achiever, you have a great deal of stamina and work hard. You take great satisfaction from being busy and productive.

- [ ] Participate in a "Year Through the Bible" program. You will feel great satisfaction and growth as you check off each day's reading and see what you have accomplished at the end of the year.

- [ ] Make a prayer list of people, events, and situations you are concerned about. Pray through this list at least once a day.

- [ ] Ask to serve in a leadership position in your parish. Your drive to achieve will help the groups you lead accomplish a great deal.

- [ ] Volunteer to organize a mission project for your parish — locally or internationally. Set goals for the mission team, and keep track of your accomplishments.

- [ ] Volunteer to be a resource for your parish's annual planning retreat. You will be able to help break down abstract dreams into achievable goals with measurable milestones.

- [ ] What is your idea of spiritual maturity? What characteristics of spiritual maturity have you seen in others? Make a list of your goals for spiritual maturity, and keep track of your progress on achieving those goals.

- [ ] You like to work hard, and you appreciate the hard work of others. When getting involved in a parish project, choose to work with other hard workers. As you and your team create common goals, you will feel great satisfaction in achieving those goals together — and create a common bond.

☐ Accept that you might be discontented even when you achieve. Because of who you are, this is God's way of nudging you forward. As you focus on your spiritual growth, your internal "need to achieve" will keep pushing you to grow.

☐ Because for you every day starts at zero, you need to remind yourself to celebrate what you have accomplished. Take a moment to appreciate your successes. You can look ahead tomorrow. Today, celebrate. Even God took time to stop and say, "It is good" multiple times when He created the universe.

☐ Be careful not to let your "list" take ultimate priority. Remember that your list is your means of achieving your goals — it is not the goal itself. Count personal achievements in your scoring "system." This will help you direct your Achiever talents toward your family, friends, and spiritual life in a positive way.

ACTIVATOR

If you are particularly talented in Activator, you can make things happen by turning thoughts into action. You are often impatient.

☐ Find a cause that really means something to you. If your parish is already involved in supporting this ministry, get involved. If it is not, you are the perfect person to get it started.

☐ Keep a log of your accomplishments each day or week. As a particularly talented Activator, you know you will be judged not by what you say, not by what you think, but by what you make happen.

☐ Consider partnering with parish friends who are exceptionally talented in Strategic, Analytical, or Futuristic. They will help you look around the corner and plan ahead.

☐ Try to work on only action-oriented teams. Typical parish committees will bore you. Your sense of urgency can be a key factor in effecting change.

☐ Take responsibility for your intensity by always asking for action when you are part of a group. You have the talent to help a group work around obstacles.

☐ If you have exceptional Relator or Woo talents along with your Activator, you may be an excellent recruiter for your parish ministry teams or adult faith formation classes.

☐ Seek opportunities to make your own decisions and act on them. In particular, look for start-up situations, like beginning a new ministry, program, or class. You also can be helpful in reviving programs that have lost their spark but are still important to the mission of your parish.

☐ Your spiritual growth will come more from doing than from discussing or thinking. Recognize that traditional adult religious education sessions might bore you — and don't let others make you feel guilty about it. You will grow best from putting biblical principles into action, like volunteering your time to work in a homeless shelter, going on a short-term mission trip to build a school in Central America, or working in a free clinic.

☐ Others might dismiss you as impatient and label you a "ready, fire, aim" person. So was Peter — and Jesus chose him as a leader, saying, "…you are Peter, and upon this rock I will build my church" (Matthew 16:18). Recognize, however, that you may make some mistakes along the way, and be prepared to apologize and fix them. Also consider partnering with people who are particularly talented in themes such as Strategic, Deliberative, or Responsibility. Their talents can help you prevent these mistakes.

☐ Recognize that your "pushiness" might sometimes intimidate others. You can soften this by remembering that it is through relationships that God works best: Don't let your desire for action ruin your relationships.

ADAPTABILITY

If you are particularly talented in Adaptability, you prefer to "go with the flow." You tend to be a "now" person who takes things as they come and discovers the future one day at a time.

- ☐ You like change. You might be at your best when you take on short-term, spur-of-the-moment roles in the parish that need to be filled quickly. One week, you might give a regular Catechism teacher a break by agreeing to substitute, and the next week might find you volunteering to serve refreshments following a funeral, or offering your basement floor to an out-of-state youth group that needs a place to sleep.

- ☐ Many people see last-minute requests as interruptions. Being the adaptable person that you are, you see them as beautifully disguised opportunities for service. Let people know that it is never too late to ask for your help.

- ☐ You live in the moment. Not yesterday, not tomorrow — *today*. You want to be fully immersed in the here and now. In order for you to grow, you need to focus on how your faith is lived in each moment. It is not reflections on the past or discussions about the future, but the experiences of the present that make your heart beat fast.

- ☐ Don't make commitments that are too far into the future. The further you are from the present, the less you are likely to be engaged. What occasionally looks like procrastination might actually be your high levels of Adaptability talent.

☐ Your best service will be in your parish's most dynamic and changing environments. Depending on your other dominant areas of talent, it could be caring for toddlers in the nursery, directing traffic in the parish parking lot, fielding calls on a 24-hour suicide hotline, or taking care of customers at your parish's food pantry.

☐ While you don't necessarily have a strong preoccupation with or appreciation for tomorrow, your ability to fully experience the present may assist those who are planning and preparing for the future. Your keen awareness of the present situation can help clarify their plans for future improvement.

☐ Avoid roles in your parish that demand structure and predictability. These roles will quickly frustrate you, make you feel inadequate, stifle your independence — and limit your opportunities to do what you do best.

☐ Cultivate your reputation as a calm and reassuring person when others become upset by daily events. Because change is your "friend," you can help others adapt to and live with the changes that are bound to come into their lives.

☐ Help those around you appreciate the moment. Help them treasure the present as a precious gift from God. God is not just God of the past and future, but also God of the present. Eternity begins now.

☐ As you read the scriptures, pay particular attention to the times when God surprises people. You will understand the wonder and joy such surprises can bring, and reading about the God of surprising change will deepen your faith and enhance your spiritual journey.

ANALYTICAL

If you are particularly talented in Analytical, you search for reasons and causes. You have the ability to think about all the factors that might affect a situation.

☐ Look for tangible evidence and data that validate your faith. Develop a logical explanation that can be shared with others who seek the truth.

☐ Develop your question-asking talents. Great questions could lead you to great personal and spiritual discoveries.

☐ Participate in a parish ministry that not only allows, but even encourages you to blend your faith and your intellect.

☐ You are more apt to act with commitment when you are convinced of something. Ask questions and do research that will help you to give a definitive *yes* or *no*.

☐ When a situation is charged with emotion, offer the logic of your cool head.

☐ Don't be afraid to express your skepticism. It will bring validity and reality to any discussion of what could be. Make sure your analysis is delivered in a positive and helpful manner.

☐ Intensely research a faith concept or topic that is personally relevant and that you are passionate about. By thoroughly analyzing the subject, your faith will grow stronger and deeper.

☐ You long to see improvement and growth in your parish, but in your mind such progress will never be the result of jumping to conclusions or jumping on the bandwagon. You can help others take a more thoughtful, responsible, and organized approach to the future.

☐ Continue to use your Analytical talents to think about the important numbers in your parish. What patterns or trends are obvious to you? When you are convinced of something, you tend to become a committed and articulate advocate.

☐ When serving in decision-making roles in your parish, identify credible, reliable sources. You are at your best when you have well-researched sources of information and numbers to support your logic. For example, determine the most helpful books, Web sites, or publications that can serve as references.

ARRANGER

If you are particularly talented in Arranger, you can organize, but you also have a flexibility that complements this ability. You like to figure out how all of the pieces and resources can be arranged for maximum productivity.

☐ Think about all that God enables you to be a part of. Think about all that you accomplish in a day. Take the time to thank God for helping you do all that you do.

☐ How many different things do you like to have going on at one time? How much can you take on in the parish and still be effective? You love to "juggle," but to ensure that you maintain quality, know the volume of projects or responsibilities you can handle and still maintain quality.

☐ Volunteer your multitasking abilities. Serve on parish committees that take on large projects you can help manage. With your ability to see the most efficient way to complete projects, you may not be happy simply carrying out others' tasks. Join a steering committee or group that helps make decisions.

☐ How can you help someone who is overwhelmed by all of his or her tasks? Help bring calm to people or situations. Let them know how you envision things working out. You may see it more clearly than they are able to.

☐ Your talent with logistics could make you very helpful in running the operations for your parish. Seek roles in these areas.

☐ If you are talented in working with numbers, consider volunteering to work with the financial operations of your parish. Your Arranger talents can help you find ways to make sure projects and programs can happen without financial obstacles.

☐ The fact that you are flexible doesn't mean that your priorities and values are constantly changing. When challenged, explain that your values and priorities remain the same, but that you are simply looking for better ways to implement them.

☐ Know and understand the mission, vision, and values of your parish. With your talents, you can help your parish pastors find new and better ways to more effectively accomplish the mission.

☐ Your spiritual growth probably won't follow a set routine, even though you may make daily time for your growth. You will constantly try different methods, programs, and strategies, finding what works best for you at the moment. As your life circumstances change, however, so will your spiritual growth practices.

☐ As you read the scriptures, pay particular attention to stories of how God and others find a "better way." From Creation to Covenant, from Cross to Resurrection, from the apostle Paul to a "new heaven and earth," the Bible is full of examples of finding better ways to reach individuals with God's life-changing love. Your strengths and your spiritual growth will be affirmed by these stories.

BELIEF

If you are particularly talented in Belief, you have certain core values that are unchanging. Out of these values emerges a defined purpose for your life.

- [ ] How much of your day, week, month, or year is spent on those things you value? Reflect on how your beliefs affect the way you prioritize your time.

- [ ] Your faith in the things you value and believe is reassuring to others who may have doubts or who are indecisive. Spend time sharing your views with others in a nonthreatening way.

- [ ] Do your values affect your job? Working for a religious organization that promotes and shares your beliefs would enable you to freely express and live your values. Avoid any occupation or company that is inconsistent with your values or would force you to compromise them.

- [ ] What principles and values has the Bible reinforced for you? Write down the five most important lessons you've learned from the stories of the Bible. Ask others close to you to write down their list, and share your similarities and differences.

- [ ] Walk the talk. In the last 24 hours, how did you live out the purpose you were put on Earth for? In the next 24 hours, how will you live out the purpose God intended for you?

- [ ] Think about a particular spiritual speaker or homily that helped solidify your beliefs. What did this experience teach you? How was the message delivered? Share that lesson and the message with someone who might be unclear in his or her faith.

☐ Think about a specific situation in which someone held a view different from your own. How did you respond? Are you inquisitive, accepting, judging, critical? How can you be firm in your own beliefs without putting down those of others?

☐ Who is a spiritual role model for you? What do you admire about this person? Think about how you can be a spiritual role model for others, and take steps to do exactly that.

☐ Clarify your values by thinking about one of your best days ever. How did your values play into the satisfaction that you received from your best day? How can you organize your life to repeat that day as often as possible?

☐ Discover the circumstances in which you feel most comfortable sharing your strongest beliefs. Would you be best able to share your core beliefs by being a parish leader or Catechism teacher or by participating in a short-term mission project? Are the ways you are serving your parish consistent with your deepest beliefs about the most effective way to witness your faith?

COMMAND

If you are particularly talented in Command, you have presence. You can take control of a situation and make decisions.

☐ When the going gets tough, the tough get going. If a crisis or conflict emerges in your parish, get involved. People will probably look to you in times like these, and tough times will often bring out the best in you.

☐ Look for opportunities to lead. You are likely to be most comfortable and effective in the driver's seat. Others will follow you because your emotional strength provides confidence and inspiration, and your decision-making capacity will often provide clarity and direction.

☐ You will often have the courage to say what others only dare to think. In your mind, things are easier to deal with when they are up front and out in the open, so you tell it like it is. Think about situations in which the truth must be told. You are probably one of the people best equipped to tell it.

☐ You have a natural emotional power that can be explosive, that is, the power to move undesirable obstacles and barriers out of the way. Explosions can be constructive or destructive. A constructive explosion moves things that are stuck or impeding progress. What obstacles and barriers are impeding the progress of a person's faith or of your parish's ministry? Where could you detonate a strategically placed explosion?

☐ As someone who knows how to get tough, you might want to think about how you can occasionally add some tenderness to your toughness. Not every situation will be a crisis or a conflict that requires the explosiveness of your emotional power and intensity. Do you have other talents that will complement your courage with tenderness and keep your assertiveness from turning aggressive or offensive?

☐ Study some of the stories in the Bible that teach about courage and cowardice. They will help you understand the value of the gift you have and the responsibilities that come with it.

☐ Ask people for their opinions. Sometimes your candor will prove intimidating, causing others to tread very lightly for fear of your reaction. Watch for this. If necessary, explain that you are candid simply because it feels so uncomfortable to keep things bottled up, not because you want to frighten other people into silence.

☐ Take opportunities in your parish to speak plainly and directly about sensitive subjects. Your unwillingness to hide from the truth can become a source of strength and constancy for others in your parish. Strive to become known as a candid person.

☐ Find a cause you believe in and support it. You might discover yourself at your best when you are defending a cause in the face of resistance.

☐ With Command comes presence. You can make people believe they can do what others say is impossible. Your Command talents can be valuable assets in times when your parish is called on to reach a lofty goal.

COMMUNICATION

If you are particularly talented in Communication, you generally find it easy to put thoughts into words. You are a good conversationalist and presenter.

☐ Volunteer to communicate your parish leadership's vision for the future to the rest of the members of your parish. Your ability to paint the future in a story will transcend the details that others dwell on and will inspire the audience to commitment and action.

☐ As part of your spiritual growth plan, keep a journal. Each day, record the way you saw God at work in your life. Your talents will enable you to give vivid details of God's activity in everyday events.

☐ Ask to be a lector. Using the same talent with which you make your everyday stories rich and colorful, bring life and excitement to the story or passage you are asked to recite.

☐ For you, the best way to share your faith with others is through stories — stories of how you have seen God work in your life and in others' lives. Share your beliefs through stories that could be told for generations to come.

☐ The Bible is full of colorful, dramatic stories. Read them, learn them, and claim them as gems for your treasure chest. Remember them, tell them, and muse upon them when your life takes on a similar hue. They will most certainly serve as a source of comfort, encouragement, and inspiration to you.

☐ If your Communication talents are expressed through writing, volunteer to write devotional pieces in the parish bulletin or monthly newsletter. Your talents will help others deepen their faith and commitment.

☐ Practice your presentations. Your opportunities to speak about matters of faith are of utmost importance. Improvisation has a certain appeal, but in general, an audience will respond best to a presenter who knows where he or she is headed. Counterintuitively, the more prepared you are, the more natural your improvisations will appear.

☐ Volunteer to collect stories and illustrations for your pastor to use in homilies. Find out the homily topics for the month, and find stories that relate to the central themes.

☐ Often, an idea or a plan is best understood through a story. You can be the one to break up the "logjams" in parish meetings by telling a story that encapsulates the essential points of the plan and enables people to move forward.

☐ Start a collection of stories or phrases that resonate with you. For example, cut out magazine articles that move you, or write down powerful word combinations. Practice telling these stories or saying these words by yourself, out loud. Listen to yourself actually saying the words. Refine.

COMPETITION

If you are particularly talented in Competition, you measure your progress against the performance of others. You strive to win first place and revel in contests.

☐ Develop a method to measure, count, or rank your spiritual growth.

☐ Think of your spiritual life as a race. Where are you in the race? Who ahead of you would you like to catch? What will it take?

☐ Keep a journal to record your personal spiritual victories.

☐ Use your drive to win to secure an important victory over injustice or evil.

☐ Keep track of the spiritual victories in your parish and make them public. In your world, there is no victory without celebration.

☐ You know that progress must be measured to be meaningful. That's why you may be a key contributor as your parish determines its most important measures of effectiveness. After the benchmarks have been determined, you can help your parish improve by measuring against those benchmarks.

☐ Resist the temptation to assess your value — and that of others — by comparing your talents with theirs. We are each created in the image of God, and each person's talents are a valuable asset to your parish, whether they are in setting and exceeding goals or in tuning into the feelings of someone who is hurting.

☐ Let people know that being competitive does not equate with putting other people down. Your competitiveness can raise everyone's level of performance, focusing them on doing something great for God.

☐ Help your parish identify its true competition. Who or what are you fighting to defeat, and who or what are you striving to catch and emulate?

☐ Take a group of your parishioners to a parish in your area that is considered a leader in some aspect of the faith. Compare their situation to yours, and help your parish develop ways to improve.

CONNECTEDNESS

If you are particularly talented in Connectedness, you have faith in the links between all things. You believe there are few coincidences and that almost every event has a reason.

☐ Serve as the interfaith link between prayer groups in your community. In a spirit of ecumenism, exchange prayer requests. Enlist Catholics and Protestants to pray for one another's needs, for understanding that goes beyond tolerance, and for peace in the world.

☐ Pray for peace, first in your own heart, then in the hearts of your brothers and sisters — especially those whose decisions dramatically influence the lives of others. Include leaders of nations, armies, and diplomatic corps.

☐ Join or start a prayer ministry in your parish. Pray for those who request prayers for themselves, their family, their friends, and for the entire human family.

☐ Create a solitude experience. Spend one day, a weekend, a week, or more away from the distractions of daily life. During your time away, simply "be." Slow down. Look. Listen. Notice. Seek God in this sacred quiet space.

☐ Visit members of your parish who cannot attend Mass. Reach out to the homebound, nursing home residents, the sick, the overwhelmed caregiver, the single parent, or the unemployed. Simply spend quality time with them. Listen attentively; be present.

☐ Explore leading a Bible study group. Your Connectedness talents might naturally equip you to see connections between the Biblical world and the modern world and to readily perceive ancient lessons that are still applicable today.

☐ Pay attention to print and broadcast media for news about people around the world or in your community who are suffering, struggling, grieving, rescuing, or providing medical assistance and humanitarian aid. Remember these people in your daily prayers as you go about your studies, work, play, or relaxation.

☐ Communicate by telephone, e-mail, or mail with members of your parish who are in the military, imprisoned, away at school, or for other reasons temporarily living far from their home parish. You can help them feel connected even when they are not physically present.

☐ Start or expand a recycling program or a soil or water conservation program in your parish. This is a way for you to put your understanding of our connection to the environment into action.

☐ Organize or participate in a blood drive in your parish. Giving blood is a relatively simple act with far-reaching consequences, saving lives of people you may never know.

CONSISTENCY

If you are particularly talented in Consistency, you are keenly aware of the need to treat people the same. You try to treat everyone in the world with consistency by setting up clear rules and adhering to them.

☐ Make a list of the rules of consistency by which you can live — your own set of "spiritual laws." These rules might be based on certain values that you have or on certain truths that you consider "non-negotiables" in your Catholic faith. Counterintuitively, the clearer these rules, the more comfortable you will be with individuality within these boundaries.

☐ You will grow best in a faith environment where expectations are clearly defined and rules are equally enforced. How would you characterize your parish with regard to expectations and rules?

☐ To you, rules are not heavy burdens, but helpful blessings. They keep you on the right track. What are the most critical rules that you follow to keep you on track spiritually?

☐ You are likely to have a higher standard than most with regard to keeping the rules. You may need to occasionally remind yourself that relationships are more important than rules and that rules are a means, not an end in themselves.

☐ You think people should be treated the same, and you are sensitive to inequality and injustice. Do you know someone in your community or parish whose rights have been violated because of race, gender, age, socio-economic status, or education? How could you be an advocate for this person or group?

☐ You probably will be more at home in situations and settings where concrete tasks are accomplished or policy decisions are being made instead of places where theoretical, abstract, or long-range discussions are taking place.

☐ You are better at thinking about the group than thinking about the individual. You see the forest better than you see the trees. Use your awareness of equality in the midst of diversity to help develop organizational policies and procedures that create a level playing field in your parish.

☐ You think people should be treated the same. Could there be some exceptions to the rule? In what instances might individualization be more valuable than generalization? When might it be okay to say, "It depends"?

☐ Balanced and consistent, your even-keeled approach could have a calming and supportive effect on those who live chaotic lives. You might be a stable and solid pillar on whom others can lean.

☐ Cultivate a reputation in your parish for pinpointing those who really deserve credit. Ensure that respect is always given to those who truly performed the work. You can become known as the conscience of your parish.

CONTEXT

If you are particularly talented in Context, you enjoy thinking about the past. You understand the present by researching its history.

☐ Think back to what you were taught about God as a child. Ponder these questions: In what ways has your image of God remained basically the same? In what ways is it quite different?

☐ Study the history of your Catholic faith, examining the lives of its popes and saints. How do their trials and tribulations, as well as their trust and faith in God, give you a model for how to live your life in the 21ˢᵗ century?

☐ Write your spiritual autobiography. Include photos of key events in your life. Create a timeline to illustrate turning points in your unique spiritual journey.

☐ Research the history of your parish. Work alone or with others to write an account of that history. Interview the oldest members to capture their earliest memories of their parish. Collect photographs, newsletters, bulletins, architectural plans, member directories, and lists of pastors and other leaders. Consider publishing and selling this history as a fundraising project.

☐ Identify strained relationships or misunderstandings between individuals or groups within your parish. As a first step toward reconciliation, identify and understand the events and factors that contributed to their discomfort with each other. By truly listening and helping them understand how they arrived at their conflict, you can help individuals and groups resolve their differences.

☐ Serve on your parish's anniversary celebration committee. Record living histories on audiotape, videotape, or DVD. Interview members of all ages as they prepare for, participate in, and remember the anniversary's events and their meanings.

☐ Teach or participate in a class that studies current events and relates those events to issues of faith. You will enjoy researching the history of the event to understand "how we got here," and sharing your knowledge with others will bring richness to the discussion.

☐ If you are teaching a class or leading a small group, build your lessons around case studies and stories from the Bible. You will enjoy the search for the appropriate case or Bible story, and those you teach will learn from these precedents. Use your understanding of the past to help others map the future.

☐ In your study of the Bible, be sure to read books about the history of the Bible — for example, the discovery of ancient texts; the ancient culture of the Middle East; and how the Bible was authored, edited, and codified. Understanding the Bible's historical context will deepen your appreciation of the Bible's message for today.

☐ Be ready to accept change. Remember that God is not just the God of the past, but also of the present and the future. Context does not equate with "living in the past." Instead, you can actually become known as an active agent for positive change. Your Context talents should allow you to identify more clearly than most the aspects of the past that can be discarded and those that must be retained to build a sustainable future.

DELIBERATIVE

If you are particularly talented in Deliberative, you are best described by the serious care you take in making decisions or choices. You anticipate the obstacles.

- ☐ Identify the threats that could destroy your spiritual health or inhibit your growth. Take careful steps to come up with a plan that will protect you from those threats.

- ☐ Figure out how much time you need to make important personal decisions. Study one of your most successful decisions. What factors contributed to the success of that decision? Seek to replicate these factors in future decision making.

- ☐ Be a resource to groups that make important decisions. You can identify potential risks and pitfalls.

- ☐ Help others slow down long enough to consider all of the important details and factors that go into wise and responsible decision making.

- ☐ Intentionally play the role of "devil's advocate." Your questions will cause others to think and will ensure better decisions.

- ☐ Be intentional about getting to know those you live near or work closely with. Don't allow your cautious style to isolate you from relationships. This will take time for you, so make sure you allow for it.

- ☐ You believe that an ounce of prevention is worth a pound of cure. Consequently, you will usually be better at preventing than promoting. You are more apt to be guilty of sins of omission than sins of commission, so be careful not to let your cautious nature prevent you from taking action when you need to.

☐ Sometimes individuals and organizations lack restraint. That can be dangerous. You can be the brakes that slow down and prevent someone or something from a tragic crash.

☐ During times of change in your parish, consider the advantages of being conservative when making decisions. Be ready to explain these advantages to others when asked.

☐ Whatever your role, take responsibility for helping others think through their decisions. Because you see details that others do not, you will soon be sought as a valuable sounding board.

DEVELOPER

If you are particularly talented in Developer, you recognize and cultivate the potential in others. You spot the signs of each small improvement and derive satisfaction from these improvements.

- ☐ You usually like it when others come to you for advice. Find positions in which you can be seen as a counselor to feed this internal need.

- ☐ Identify the people in your parish or spiritual groups whom you have helped. Tell them of the joy you received from helping them, and remind them that you are there for them in the future.

- ☐ Identify others who you believe are good "teachers." Ask them how they encourage others to grow and achieve. Try incorporating their methods into your own as you seek to build strengths as a developer.

- ☐ Think about the people in your parish's adult religious education sessions or study groups whom you have seen succeed or achieve milestones. Recognize them for their accomplishments, and help them think of new goals to strive for.

- ☐ How can you help your parish, as a whole, develop? Ask your parish priests about their goals. Encourage and recognize them for leading the development of your parish.

- ☐ If you like working with children, pick a Catechism class to teach or assist. Would you enjoy being a youth group teacher or assistant? Think about how much joy you would receive seeing the spiritual development of your students.

☐ Ask your pastors if there is a person in your parish who could benefit from a spiritual mentor. Just having one-on-one time might be helpful to that person.

☐ List the last five people you have encouraged. Why did you encourage them? What motivated you? What methods of encouragement worked best? Learn from your successes.

☐ Find a way to mark progress in your spiritual growth. You will derive satisfaction as you see your progress because you know that even small steps in the right direction can yield big results over time.

☐ Because you are "wired" to notice progress in people, your pastor could benefit from your encouragement. Pastors sometimes feel that they see very little fruit of their efforts, and you have the talent to show your pastor how he is succeeding — even when success is not readily apparent.

DISCIPLINE

If you are particularly talented in Discipline, you enjoy routine and structure. Your world is best described by the order you create.

☐ Volunteer to be part of a cleaning day at your parish. Help bring neatness and order to the area you are assigned.

☐ Volunteer to create a timeline, including celebrations of milestones for major projects in your parish, such as a building fund campaign, Catechism attendance recognition, or a "paintathon."

☐ Volunteer to keep the parish calendar of events current and accurate.

☐ Make Bible reading and prayer part of your daily routine. You'll come to love the predictability, and you will grow spiritually as a result.

☐ As you study the scriptures, look for times when God brought order out of chaos. You'll see it in Genesis at the Creation, and you will see it all the way through to Revelation, when God returns to claim His own out of worldly chaos.

☐ Volunteer to help keep or organize your parish's records. Your Discipline talents will make preparing the annual report much easier. In fact, you may enjoy preparing the report, gathering and organizing all the information so that it is a coherent whole.

☐ Recognize that mistakes might depress you. Precision is a core part of who you are; however, you must find ways to move through these moments of annoyance to prevent becoming discouraged.

☐ Recognize that others may not be as disciplined as you are. Sometimes, their processes will seem clumsy and disorganized to you. Try to look beyond the processes, and instead assess the results. Remember that even though God brought order out of chaos in Creation, the crowning achievement of Creation was fallible, unpredictable human beings.

☐ Learn the art of forgiveness, especially the art of forgiving yourself. Even though perfection is your goal, accept the fact that you and others will rarely reach perfection. Forgive and move on, celebrating the excellence achieved in spite of imperfection.

☐ Choose to serve on committees and join groups in the parish that have structure and established routines. Groups and committees without well-defined processes and expectations will frustrate you.

EMPATHY

If you are particularly talented in Empathy, you can sense the feelings of other people by imagining yourself in others' lives or others' situations.

☐ Appreciate your gift for getting in touch with the thoughts and feelings of others. You can naturally build trust with others by telling them that you know how they are feeling.

☐ Spend time in silent prayer. It provides the potential for you to look within your soul and to experience your inner being. Simply observe your emotions and what goes on in your mind.

☐ Mass can be more than just a ritual for you. Allow yourself to get in touch with the emotional aspects of the prayers, the hymns, the Eucharist. Your emotional connection will make Christ's presence real to you.

☐ Learn to recognize your own signs of being overly stressed, and know what to do about it. It is essential that you know when and how to make yourself a priority.

☐ Because you instinctively tune in to the feelings of others, you can assist those who have experiences of loss through death, divorce, or illness.

☐ Take the time to help, whether it's a stranger who needs directions, a child who needs extra attention learning how to read, or your aging neighbor who can't carry his groceries.

☐ Sponsor a child in a developing country. There are several organizations that coordinate such efforts. Ask your pastor for details.

☐ Know your limits. Don't push yourself beyond the healthy zone or the sanity zone. Keeping yourself in balance by knowing your limits is a big step toward keeping the world at large in balance.

☐ Jot down prayers and record insights from Bible readings. You may find that as you write, you hear God speaking in ways you had not heard before.

☐ Sometimes it is important to be silent. You have the talent to let other people understand that you know how they are feeling without talking. Over time, refine your nonverbal communication skills.

FOCUS

If you are particularly talented in Focus, you can take a direction, follow through, and make the corrections necessary to stay on track. You prioritize, then act.

☐ Start every day by giving thanks for all the people whose lives you will touch and whose lives will touch yours — from up-close or from a distance.

☐ Express gratitude for one, two, or three things that positively affected you during the day. Even on the worst of days, ask God to help you know when He was present in your life that day. This will help you refocus on the positive aspects of your life — aspects that in the long run will make you more effective.

☐ Participate in a "Year Through the Bible" program. You will feel great satisfaction and growth as you follow through on your commitment and see what you have accomplished at the end of the year.

☐ Volunteer to serve on committees or task forces that are charged with accomplishing a vast, complex goal. Your Focus talents will help others see the pertinent issues and keep the team on track.

☐ What are your goals for spiritual growth in the coming week, month, or year? Are the things you are doing and the way you are living helping you accomplish your goals? Your ability to prioritize will help you see the steps you need to take to reach your goal — eliminating the "excess baggage" along the way.

☐ Volunteer to serve on your parish's outreach team. You will be able to help define goals for growth and set the priorities that will help the team reach those goals.

☐ Make a habit of praying at the same time each day. Whether it is five minutes or 50 minutes, set aside this time for yourself and God. Let prayer take a form that fits your style. Be open to changing how you use this time if you need variety. The key is to make a habit of fitting God into your day, whether it is in your quiet place at home, riding your bike, commuting to work, washing the dishes, or drinking a cup of coffee.

☐ Your greatest worth as a member of one of your parish's teams or committees might be to help others set goals. At the end of each meeting, take responsibility for summarizing what was decided, for defining when these decisions will be acted on, and for setting a date when the group will reconvene.

☐ Take the time to write down your goals for spiritual growth, and refer to them often. You will feel more in control of your life this way. When you set your goals, discipline yourself to attach timelines and measurements. These will provide regular proof that you are indeed making progress.

☐ Identify your role models and "heroes of the faith." Write down in detail why you want to focus your life on similar kinds of actions, attitudes, and faithfulness.

FUTURISTIC

If you are particularly talented in Futuristic, you are inspired by the future and what could be. You inspire others with your visions of the future.

☐ Start or join a regular discussion of the future of your parish. Ask others who are especially talented in Futuristic to join you. Meet once a month just to talk about the possibilities of your parish's future. Be sure to include some people with exceptional Activator, Achiever, or Focus talents so your shared vision can become a reality.

☐ Study the Bible, paying attention to God's promises related to the future — for your future, for future generations, for the future of the Church.

☐ Volunteer to talk about what you see as the future of your parish. Your vision of the possibilities ahead will inspire others.

☐ Offer to help those who are experiencing difficult times. You can help them see a future of possibilities instead of the overwhelming present.

☐ When your parish undertakes an ambitious project (like a building program) or is going through a major change (like a new pastor), you can set people's minds at ease by painting a vivid, hopeful picture of the future as a result of the project or change.

☐ Your vision of the future motivates you to work toward creating it, but remember that the future ultimately belongs to God. The disciples most certainly did not envision being called by Jesus, but God had other plans — and the disciples were open to the possibilities. Be proactive as you travel the road to your future, but be prepared for surprises God may present along the way — and be open to changing your plans.

☐ When you have an opportunity to describe your parish's future in an article or a presentation, use as much detail as possible. Not everyone can intuitively see the future as clearly as you can.

☐ Don't get so wrapped up in thinking about and living in the promise of the future that you fail to appreciate the wonder of today. God is the God of all time and wants you to celebrate the present as well as plan for the future.

☐ When meetings get bogged down in "we've never done it that way before" talk, your vision of future possibilities can be a source of motivation for the group. The more vividly and hopefully you describe the future, the better people are able to move out of the past.

☐ Keep pictures, books, notes, or other reminders of what you are working toward where you will see them frequently. This will help you focus your talents and more effectively achieve your goals.

HARMONY

If you are particularly talented in Harmony, you look for consensus. You don't enjoy conflict; rather, you seek areas of agreement.

☐ You may experience spiritual satisfaction and growth by being involved in hands-on, practical projects in your parish.

☐ While some people are energized by conflict and confrontation, such discord will cause you discomfort. You will flourish more with teachers and mentors who have a considerate and cooperative approach to learning than with those who tend to stir up controversy and rely on debate.

☐ You have a knack for smoothing out the bumps and creating more harmonious environments. How do you do this now? How could you do it better?

☐ Remember that harmony, not uniformity, is your goal. You instinctively understand that harmony cannot occur if everyone is "singing the same note." Help the people in the "choir" hear and appreciate the different parts that people "sing."

☐ You can see the common ground that links conflicted people. Be a key person in helping others understand what they already agree on. You will be more likely than others to notice commonalities.

☐ You are likely to be most open to growth when your life is balanced. Strive for internal harmony that exists between the competing demands and roles of your life.

☐ When you disagree with someone, you might find it difficult to express your thoughts and feelings. When is it most difficult for

191

you to "speak the truth in love"? When is the truth more important than peace?

☐ You are sensitive to conflict. Who are the conflicted people around you? What are the conflicted areas in your parish? Who might this information be important to?

☐ Don't let people in your parish waste time and energy debating at the expense of important practical matters that must be taken care of. Your Harmony talents can help others focus on the truly important things about which they agree.

☐ Use your Harmony talents to build a network of people with differing perspectives that you can rely on when you need expertise. Your openness to these differing perspectives will help you learn.

IDEATION

If you are particularly talented in Ideation, you are fascinated by ideas. You are able to find connections between seemingly disparate phenomena.

☐ Write your own prayers to mark your joys and sorrows as well as your successes and failures. Jot down the date. Collect your favorite personal prayers and put them into a book.

☐ Spend time "musing" on spiritual things each day. This thinking time is very valuable to your growth, as your creative mind will find new ways to connect God to everyday living.

☐ Offer to teach a class that explores different religious traditions. Your Ideation talents will enable you to explain the complexities of these traditions clearly, and they will also help you see the connections between them.

☐ You will be a valuable member of any group, committee, or team that is charged with finding new ways to do things — from community outreach, to redefining the parish's organizational structure, to creating a new approach to teaching Christian formation classes. Your ability to help others see things from a different angle will help create new possibilities.

☐ As you study the scriptures, look for stories of innovation — the new "big ideas" that God introduced at different times in history. Seek to understand why the Christian movement was such a radical departure from the traditions of the time — and find an opportunity to share these insights with others.

☐ Whenever there is a disagreement or "logjam" in your parish, you can help get things unstuck by looking at the situation from a

193

different perspective, finding alternate solutions, and sharing what you see with those in leadership.

☐ Volunteer to help your pastor create meaningful services and liturgies for special celebrations and feast days in your parish. Weave a tapestry of music, readings, symbols, and quiet reflection time as well as prayers of praise, thanksgiving, and petition.

☐ Establish a practice of frequently journaling with God. Make this experience sacred by having a special journal and pen used only for this time with God. Dialogue with God — openly and honestly, trusting what flows from your pen onto the pages of your journal. Every couple of months, flip through your journal and read various entries. Look for recurring patterns, problems solved, and what created peace within you.

☐ Seek brainstorming sessions. There are bound to be teams in your parish that are charged with creating new ways or improving existing ways of doing things — building maintenance committees, strategic planning teams, outreach and mission teams, to name a few. With your abundance of ideas, you will make these sessions more exciting and more productive.

☐ You can become bored quickly, so make small changes in your spiritual life and your involvement in parish activities and service opportunities. Experiment — try different ways of praying, attend a Mass that is a different style than the one you typically attend, get involved in a ministry that you've never done before. All of these will help keep you stimulated.

INCLUDER

If you are particularly talented in Includer, you are accepting of others. You show awareness of those who feel left out, and you make an effort to include them.

☐ For you, the Church is never an exclusive club for the chosen few. It is always an inclusive community where everyone is welcome. You might consider using your Includer talents to actively contact and welcome those outside your parish and invite them to visit.

☐ When an outsider does come to your parish, consider using your Includer talents to introduce this new person to some of the existing members. You instinctively know that nothing makes an outsider feel more at home than knowing someone's name and having someone know his.

☐ As an Includer, you know that the best way to become a part of something is to get involved in it. You may play a key role in helping new people in your parish move from spectators to participants, from consumers to contributors. You might be the perfect person to be involved in a newcomers' class designed to help individuals find their place.

☐ Your Includer talents may have more of a global, rather than local, flavor. You know that "God so loved the world" and that Jesus said, "Go into all the world." You have sensitivity toward those who may be left out. You might play a key role in encouraging diversity in the parish by becoming a member of your parish's mission team. Skin color, language, gender, age, or race should never keep people outside and apart from God.

☐ You probably have an instinctive awareness of exclusion. You know what it feels like to be left out. This awareness and understanding could be valuable to those who seek to create a more open and welcoming environment in their parish, their class, or their small group. Maybe you could teach a class on the subject or let others know of your willingness to consult individually.

☐ Volunteer to assist with the implementation of a parish-wide survey. As an Includer, you want every voice to be heard, and a survey is a great way to make that happen.

☐ Whenever you go to a parish event or meeting, consider yourself to be the designated greeter. Make it a point to talk to a new person before you talk to a friend or an acquaintance. This will probably come easily for you, and it will pull newcomers in.

☐ You naturally look for the best in people. Help your friends and fellow members see what you see: that we are all created in the image of God and that God loves and values everyone.

☐ You might be a great advocate for global missions because you can see and explain what we all have in common. You can help others understand that to respect the differences among us (our diversity), you must begin by appreciating what we all share (our similarity).

☐ As you study the scriptures, pay particular attention to the stories and instances in which God and others welcome strangers and are advocates of the poor and oppressed. These passages will resonate with you, and your spiritual growth will be enriched by the God who is the friend of the poor and who welcomes the stranger.

INDIVIDUALIZATION

If you are particularly talented in Individualization, you are intrigued with the unique qualities of each person. You have a gift for figuring out how people who are different can work together productively.

☐ Establish a study group composed of people who possess different perspectives and different beliefs. The differences will fascinate you, and you will enjoy expanding your own viewpoints.

☐ Become a mentor to new members of your parish. You have a knack for spotting what each new member enjoys, desires, and needs, and you can help each of them follow their own paths.

☐ Offer to be a task force leader. It is easy for you to figure out the right roles for each person based on individual talents and strengths.

☐ Become an expert in describing your own talents and strengths. What is the best way to grow in your faith? How do you learn best? Recognizing your own individuality will help you recognize others' uniqueness.

☐ Read the biographies of great spiritual leaders — or of ordinary people who have triumphed over impossible odds. You will be able to see how their unique talents made them successful.

☐ Offer to teach a class on the "great characters of the Bible." Your Individualization talents will make these characters come alive for your class.

☐ Your ability to see people one by one is a talent. Seek out opportunities to serve and lead in your parish in which your Individualization talents can be appreciated and used. You might excel at counseling, supervising, teaching, writing human interest articles for your parish newsletter, or serving on the nominating committee.

☐ Be ready to help others understand that true diversity can be found in the subtle differences between individuals, regardless of race, sex, or nationality. Because you know that human beings are uniquely created by God, you can help people see the unique beauty in others.

☐ You may need to explain that it is appropriate, just, and effective to treat each person differently. Those with less Individualization talent might not see the differences among individuals and might insist that individualization is unequal and therefore unfair.

☐ Help your friends in your parish become aware of each other's unique talents and needs. Soon people will ask you to help them understand another person's actions and attitudes.

INPUT

If you are particularly talented in Input, you have a craving to know more. You may very well like to collect and archive all kinds of information.

☐ Consider taking a trip to the Holy Land, the Middle East, or the Mediterranean. Your faith is likely to come alive as you actually see and experience the places in biblical and Church history.

☐ Your natural inquisitiveness can help you be an outstanding researcher. Make yourself available to do research for those who need to speak or teach on topics about which they know little. Your resourcefulness will be valuable and helpful to such people as you provide them with interesting facts and relevant stories.

☐ You may already have a library of religious books and resources that have enriched your own spiritual life. Consider developing a system that will enable you to share them with others.

☐ If your parish has a library, you might enjoy volunteering there. If it doesn't, you might be a key person in getting one started.

☐ Your capacity for collecting and gathering might make you a natural contributor to your parish's newsletter or Web site. You could help inform others about what is going on both inside and outside your parish.

☐ In order to grow, you need to know. You need to know all about the Faith of which you are a part. Reading about the particulars of Catholicism, interviewing long-time members of your parish, understanding all the factors that contributed to the watershed moments of the Christian faith — these will deepen your faith and enrich your spiritual life.

☐ Accept that you will never feel that you know enough — but don't let that paralyze you into inaction. Know how to determine when you know enough to act. Partnering with someone particularly talented in Activator or Achiever will help you accomplish great things for God.

☐ You will collect things that others will eventually need — from books to ideas to parish information. Be ready to share.

☐ Identify situations in which you can share the information you have collected with other people. You could lead a small group or teach a class in your parish. If you are not the leader, you could serve as a resource to enhance the topic or lesson with the knowledge you have gathered.

☐ In your study of the scriptures, compare various translations, learning about the translation process of each edition. The variances in meaning and differences in interpretation may fascinate you and deepen your appreciation of the Bible.

INTELLECTION

If you are particularly talented in Intellection, you are characterized by your intellectual activity. You are introspective, and you appreciate intellectual discussions.

☐ Schedule regular time for reflection, introspection, or meditation. This will be a fruitful time for you.

☐ Keep a list of the most important issues you are thinking about and/or the books you are reading.

☐ Record your thoughts on important concepts or issues, or communicate them to others, either verbally or in writing. This organization will lead to greater clarification of your thoughts and will prepare them for further development.

☐ Raise the deep and philosophical questions that others may not be aware of.

☐ Volunteer to review and recommend articles and books that are important for members of your parish to read.

☐ Find partners who can help you turn your thoughts and ideas into practical and concrete action. Consider those who are especially talented in themes such as Activator, Strategic, and Achiever.

☐ Offer your thinking to primary teachers in your parish. You will help them anticipate questions and achieve greater depth in their teaching.

☐ Take a yearly retreat for an extended period of solitude. You will return energized and ready to put your thoughts into action.

☐ Record your thoughts. It will help you clarify them, and it will prompt further thinking.

☐ Use your intellect to do an in-depth study of a critical issue or problem faced by your parish.

LEARNER

If you are particularly talented in Learner, you have a great desire to learn, and you want to continuously improve. In particular, the process of learning, rather than the outcome, excites you.

☐ Participate in an adult faith formation class or Bible study class. Become an expert in your own religious beliefs and knowledgeable in the history of the Church.

☐ Feed your constant need to learn through a Bible lesson for each day of the year.

☐ Share your knowledge in group seminars and workshops for your parish or study groups.

☐ Start a book club with a religious premise. Center your group on educational and informative books about faith and spirituality. If Context is also one of your dominant areas of talent, you might also like books with a historical perspective.

☐ Keep track of what you have learned. Create a spiritual résumé of all you have learned and done. Share it with others so they may call on you as a resource.

☐ Ask what conferences or workshops are available for you to attend. Let others know you are willing to represent your parish at these programs.

☐ You can be a catalyst for change in your parish. Others might be intimidated by new ideas, new routines, or new circumstances, but your willingness to soak up this "newness" can calm their fears and spur them to participate. Take this responsibility seriously.

☐ Refine how you learn. For example, you might learn best by teaching. If so, seek opportunities in your parish to teach a class or lead a small group. You might learn best through quiet reflection; if so, carve out this quiet time and "soak up" as much as you can about God.

☐ Find ways to mark the progress of your learning. If there are distinct levels or stages of learning within your spiritual growth program or the class you are taking, celebrate your progression from one level to the next. If no such levels exist, create them for yourself (for example, read five books on the apostle Paul, or make three presentations on new trends in Christian theology).

☐ Ask your pastor what theological or parish management books he is reading, and read them as well. In doing so, you can fulfill your need to learn and also share what you've learned with your pastor, providing him with valuable feedback.

MAXIMIZER

If you are particularly talented in Maximizer, you focus on strengths as a way to stimulate personal and group excellence. You seek to transform something good into something superb.

☐ Consider how your talents and strengths relate to the mission in your life and how you can combine them to benefit your family, your parish, or your community.

☐ Avoid serving on parish committees that require continual problem solving — this will only frustrate you. You thrive not on fixing what's broken, but instead on taking what is working well and making it even better.

☐ Study success. Find out what has made the most successful parishes, spiritual leaders, and "ordinary people" succeed.

☐ When you pray, thank God for the gifts you have, and ask for insights into ways that you can best use those gifts. How can God help you reach excellence? Creating excellence in your life, in the lives of others, and in your church is your gift to God.

☐ Offer to design a program for celebrating the successes of your parish.

☐ Focus on your gifts. Are you musical? Are you a good speaker? Are you artistic? Do you love teaching others? These are your best opportunities for mastery. Consider how your gifts and talents might best benefit your parish.

☐ In group settings — committees, work teams, classes — help people recognize their own talents and strengths and those of others.

☐ Once you have identified your own talents and strengths, stay focused on them. Refine your skills, and add new ones. Acquire more knowledge. Practice. Keep working toward mastery — strength — in a few areas. Remember that God created the one and only you.

☐ Seek roles in your parish in which you are helping other people succeed. In coaching, mentoring, or teaching roles, your focus on strengths will prove particularly beneficial to others. For example, because most people find it difficult to describe what they do best, start by arming them with vivid descriptions. Help them see how God uniquely created them.

☐ Spend time with people who have discovered their talents. The more you understand how marshaling talents leads to strengths and success, the more likely you will be to create strengths and success in your own life.

POSITIVITY

If you are particularly talented in Positivity, you have an enthusiasm that is contagious. You are upbeat and can get others excited about what they are going to do.

- ☐ Seek friends who love life as much as you do. They will uplift and support you.

- ☐ People who have negative or defeating attitudes and practices can drain you, but don't avoid them or withhold your Positivity from them. They need the lift you naturally provide!

- ☐ Start a collection of stories, positive sayings, and favorite Bible verses that will keep you focused on the positive when you are facing adversity. These positive examples can also help shift the tone when parish meetings become gripe sessions.

- ☐ When others become discouraged or are reluctant to take risks, engage them in possibility thinking. Your attitude will provide the motivation to keep them moving.

- ☐ Help plan celebrations for your parish. Your Positivity talents will help the planning team focus on fun.

- ☐ Choose opportunities for service in which you can encourage others, like teaching religious education classes, mentoring new members, or prison ministry.

- ☐ When choosing study groups or classes to join, select those in which the leader has a positive attitude, and in which fun is integrated with the learning. Too much seriousness brings you down and inhibits your growth. "…for rejoicing in the LORD must be your strength!" (Nehemiah 8:10).

☐ You tend to be more enthusiastic and energetic than most people. This is a very valuable talent you can bring to the life of your parish. When others become discouraged or are reluctant to take risks, your attitude will provide the impetus to keep them moving. Over time, others will start to look to you for this "lift."

☐ Deliberately help others see God's blessings in their lives and the things that are going well for them. You can keep their eyes on the positive. Remember Paul's partner, Barnabas, whose name meant "son of encouragement" (Acts 4:36). Never underestimate the effect you can have on people.

☐ Be ready to explain that your enthusiasm is not simple naïveté. You know that bad things can happen — that there is suffering and tragedy in the world; you simply prefer to focus on the good things and on the positive ways God is working in the world. Pessimists might sometimes be right — but they are rarely the people through whom God accomplishes great things.

RELATOR

If you are particularly talented in Relator, you enjoy close relationships with others. You find deep satisfaction in working hard with friends to achieve a goal.

☐ How do you stay connected with people you have met — one on one or in groups? Be intentional about getting together or communicating with people from your parish.

☐ When you are working with others, make time to get to know them personally. Set time aside after Mass to talk with fellow parishioners. You may not be comfortable initiating conversation, so be prepared with questions to ask.

☐ Who is the friend you've known the longest? Share and discuss your feelings and beliefs about spirituality with this person.

☐ Large study or worship groups may not feel comfortable to you. Arrange for smaller, more intimate classes in which your Relator talents will flourish.

☐ Volunteer to coordinate smaller social functions for people in your parish.

☐ Remember to thank God and pray for your friends.

☐ Look for people with exceptional Woo talents in your surroundings. If you are hesitant to initiate relationships with others in your parish, they can make initial connections that you can then take deeper. Call on their talents to help you when you are in a situation with strangers or people you don't know very well.

☐ Deliberately learn as much as you can about the people that you meet in your parish. You like knowing about people, and other people like being known. You will be a catalyst for trusting relationships.

☐ Let your caring show. For example, help the members of a study group get to know each other better, or extend your relationships beyond weekend Mass.

☐ Remember that most life changes happen in relationships and that one of the cornerstones of the Christian faith is God's desire for a relationship with each and every human being. Biblical stories of deep relationships, such as that between David and Jonathan, or between Jesus and his disciples, will be particularly meaningful to you.

RESPONSIBILITY

If you are particularly talented in Responsibility, you take psychological ownership of what you say you will do. You are committed to stable values such as honesty and loyalty.

☐ You need to "live" your faith to grow spiritually. Make a commitment to perform acts of neighborly love: delivering and serving meals at a homeless shelter, volunteering at a hospital, or relieving the caregiver of a hospice patient. Choose the commitments that are most meaningful to you.

☐ Join or start an accountability group made up of individuals who commit to holding each other accountable in their walk with God. Being held accountable by others and yourself is not something you dread, but rather is something you enjoy. You will grow through your accountability.

☐ Take personal responsibility for setting aside quality time to develop your relationship with God. Find the environment and the method that resonate with you most clearly, and set aside time for them each day. You will derive much satisfaction from following through on this commitment.

☐ For you, making a financial commitment to your parish will be a powerful means of spiritual growth. Making a commitment and following through on it every week, knowing that you are funding the ministry of your parish, will be a source of satisfaction and growth for you. If you are not doing so already, consider "taking a step" each year to increase your contribution to 10% of your income, or "tithing."

☐ Be careful not to take on too much. You need to be able to follow through on each and every one of your commitments; otherwise, you will feel as if you have failed. Choose those areas of service in which you are talented and passionate.

☐ If you are also particularly talented in Woo or Activator, consider being a recruiter for various roles in your parish. Your Responsibility talents will not let you rest until each role is filled with the right person.

☐ Take time to enjoy the completion of your commitments. Responsibility is a source of motivation for you, so it is important to appreciate the successes for which you are responsible.

☐ Consider fasting as a spiritual discipline. Identify opportunities in which fasting can unite you with the world's suffering people. Besides fasting from food, consider consciously abstaining from television, shopping, or other activities you enjoy to focus your attention on "the things of God."

☐ Figure out what pulls you away from God. When you have all the best intentions to make time for daily prayer, Scripture reading, or meditation, what gets your attention instead? Work? Sleep? Television? Exercise? Shopping? Family? Friends? Household chores? Take personal responsibility for "clearing the clutter" and spending quality time with God.

☐ Start or join wellness activities in your parish. Look to the Bible for connections between taking care of your body and taking care of your spirit. Taking responsibility for your physical health is a spiritual discipline, and when you feel better, you are happier.

RESTORATIVE

If you are particularly talented in Restorative, you are adept at dealing with problems. You are good at figuring out what is wrong and resolving it.

☐ Consider being a part of the lay-counseling ministry in your parish. Tell people you are interested in their well-being and are eager to help them find solutions to their problems.

☐ Consider being a part of the lay-maintenance ministry in your parish. Use your fix-it talents in the areas of greatest expertise for you, for example, structure, plumbing, heating/cooling, or lighting.

☐ Become an advocate for the disadvantaged in your parish. Help make their needs known, and create opportunities for other members of your parish to give of their time, talent, or other resources to help these individuals.

☐ In your study of the scriptures, pay particular attention to how men and women of faith dealt with their problems. The solutions that they discovered and implemented will be inspiring to you and a resource in your restorative efforts.

☐ Help start a food bank in your parish, or arrange for contributions to your diocese's food bank.

☐ Your prayers will often focus on asking for guidance in solving problems — your own, those of others, and those of your community and world. As you open yourself up to God, you will find the solutions becoming clearer.

☐ Adopt a family in need for a period of time. Volunteer to help them get back on their feet.

☐ Your Restorative nature might lead you to be critical of your own talents. Give yourself a break, and recognize that your talents — your lesser talents as well as your greatest talents — are natural parts of you and cannot change. Try to redirect your Restorative attention toward "fixing" your areas of lesser skill and knowledge, which you *can* acquire. Accept the talents God has given you, and make the most of them.

☐ Sometimes the problems of the world's people might overwhelm you; if only you could "fix it all"! In those times, remember that the brokenness of the world cannot ultimately be fixed by you alone, but can be healed only by God.

☐ Sometimes the best way you can "fix it" is to allow other people to solve their own problems. You might want to rush in and solve things for them, but in so doing, you might hinder their learning. Often, the most important lessons we learn from God are those in which we find our own solutions.

SELF-ASSURANCE

If you are particularly talented in Self-Assurance, you feel confident in your ability to manage your own life. You possess an inner compass that gives you confidence that your decisions are right.

☐ When your internal voice speaks to you, listen. Reflect on where that instinct comes from. How does God speak to you through your own voice?

☐ Your confidence can be a source of inspiration for others. When others doubt their faith or direction, share how you came to your own decisions and beliefs.

☐ When volunteering for committees or projects, be careful of people or organizations that impose structure or direction on you. You usually don't appreciate others telling you what or how to do things.

☐ If you are also particularly talented in themes such as Communication or Belief, you may have the ability to be a powerful speaker. Discuss a passage or story from the Bible that is meaningful to you, and "persuade" others with your confidence about the lesson it teaches.

☐ Identify a person from whom you can seek spiritual advice when facing tough decisions. Because your exceptional Self-Assurance may lead you to rarely seek and always question advice, be sure this is someone who won't be offended if you don't accept his or her point of view. Honor this person by letting him or her know that you are usually very selective and rarely ask others for opinions.

☐ Do you know when to "go with God" and when to take control over those things within your power? Think about those things over which you have control and list them. Then think about those things that God has authority over. How do you let God work in your life?

☐ Think about when your intuition has been right and when it has been wrong. What was the difference? Was the "feeling" different? How can you hone your intuition?

☐ Share your Self-Assurance talents. Consider teaming with people who are especially talented in themes such as Developer, Strategic, or Futuristic, but who may not possess your high level of Self-Assurance. Your confidence can be the driving force that puts their development ideas for the church into motion.

☐ Realize that sometimes you will find it hard to put your certainty or intuition into words, possibly leading others to see you as self-righteous. Explain that your certainty does not mean that they should withhold their opinions. It might not seem like it to them, but you do want to hear their views. Your certainty at the moment doesn't mean that you are unwilling to accommodate their views.

☐ Help others find the positives in your certainty. Your Self-Assurance talents can give them confidence in God's care and providence during times of change, uncertainty, or trial.

SIGNIFICANCE

If you are particularly talented in Significance, you want to be very important in the eyes of others. You are independent and want to be recognized.

☐ Ask to help lead something big — very big — happening in your parish. You'll enjoy the opportunity to be a part of something so significant.

☐ Use your expertise to help with a special project at your parish. If you're a lawyer, be available to consult about legal advice. If you're a teacher, be available to facilitate a leaders' training event. If you're a human resources director, volunteer to chair the personnel committee.

☐ If your parish has members share their faith journeys during Mass, volunteer to share yours. Your story can inspire others.

☐ Commit to giving a tithe (10% of your income) to your parish. With a very small percentage of parishioners doing this, it sets you apart and honors God.

☐ As you study the scriptures, pay close attention to the stories of the "heroes of the faith." How did they use their extraordinary talents and gifts for the benefit of their faith communities and the world? Their stories will inspire you to greatness.

☐ Don't be afraid to dream big dreams. Ask, "If time and money were no object, what great thing would I do for God?" Then set out to accomplish it, marking your milestones along the way.

☐ Write down your Signature Themes and refer to them frequently — they are gifts from God. Heightened awareness of your talents will give you the confidence you need to rebound, when, for whatever reason, your "audiences" are not giving you the feedback you need.

☐ Remember that in the ultimate scheme of things, it is God's "applause" and not the applause of others that truly counts. Sometimes, the things that you do to further your parish's mission may go unnoticed by others — but God notices and says, "Well done, good and faithful servant." And that is all that matters.

☐ Make a list of the spiritual goals you want to achieve, and post them where you will see them every day. Use this list to inspire yourself.

☐ Accept that, unless you possess exceptional Self-Assurance talents, you might fear failure. Don't let the fear of failure cause you not to act on God's behalf. Instead, use your fear as an opportunity to fully trust in God to achieve great things through you.

STRATEGIC

If you are particularly talented in Strategic, you create alternative ways to proceed. Faced with any given scenario, you can quickly spot the relevant patterns and issues.

- ☐ Look for opportunities to "step into" and "out of" committees and task forces that have their goals defined but need help identifying the steps for reaching the goals.

- ☐ Study the Bible for insight into how men and women of faith responded to life's challenges. Then, when you are faced with similar situations, you will have additional choices from which to sort and choose. Then you can move ahead.

- ☐ There are many options available for enhancing your spiritual growth — from books, to devotionals, to Bible-reading schedules, to "10 Easy Steps to _____." With all these options in mind, find what works best for you. Follow your intuition, and don't be afraid to change your strategy as new ideas come to your attention.

- ☐ You may be a good counselor for those facing difficult decisions. You can help them weigh their options and choose the best route.

- ☐ Volunteer to serve on your parish's strategic planning team. Your natural talents will help the team consider all the possibilities and make the most productive and effective decisions about your parish's future.

- ☐ If you also have exceptional talent in themes such as Developer or Individualization, you may want to consider becoming a sponsor in your parish's Adult Catechumate. Your Strategic talents will help them see the best opportunities for growth and service, and you will grow by helping someone else grow.

☐ Jesus said, "So do not worry about tomorrow: tomorrow will take care of itself" (Matthew 6:34) (NJB). Armed with your Strategic talents, you are quick to determine the best course of action in any situation. Live at peace knowing that no matter what comes tomorrow, your God-given talents will be there to get you through.

☐ Trust your intuitive insights as often as possible. Even though you might not be able to explain them rationally, your intuitions are created by a brain that instinctively anticipates and forecasts. Have confidence in these intuitions.

☐ Musing time is essential to strategic thinking. Take the time to fully reflect or muse about a goal that your parish wants to achieve until the related patterns and issues emerge for you. Then share your insights with your parish's leaders.

☐ Talk with your pastor about the alternative directions you see that could help accomplish the parish's mission. Detailed conversations like this can be a great asset in your parish's planning processes, and they can help you become even better at anticipating possible outcomes.

WOO

If you are particularly talented in Woo, you love the challenge of meeting new people and winning them over. You derive satisfaction from breaking the ice and making a connection with another person.

☐ Join a parish study or social group of people you do not know yet. You'll enjoy the excitement of meeting new people.

☐ Be a greeter at Mass. Your Woo talents will help people feel welcome.

☐ Offer to welcome and sponsor new members in your parish. You can quickly connect with people, put them at ease, and help them feel comfortable.

☐ Be a builder of goodwill for your parish by getting to know the people who live near you. Reach out to your community. Offer to welcome new people and invite them to serve.

☐ Ask others thought-provoking questions, such as "What is the most meaningful religious experience you've had?" and engage in uplifting conversations that will help you feel connected to God in daily life.

☐ Take charge of a large social event, such as a parish fund-raising auction or dinner. Use your charm to create positive feelings.

☐ Learn the names of as many parishioners as you can. Build a card file of the people you know, and add names as you become acquainted. Include a snippet of personal information — such as their birthday, favorite color, hobby, or other personal interest.

☐ You are a natural campaigner. Is there an important project or ministry in your parish that needs a broad base of support to succeed? Use your Woo talents to bring others on board and turn a dream into reality.

☐ In group settings, take responsibility for helping put new or more reserved people at ease. Your Woo talents can help others experience your parish as warm, inviting, and accepting.

STRENGTHS STORIES

A Life-Changing Experience

A woman who has been a member of our parish for years recently joined one of our strengths development groups. This came as a surprise to us, because she always came into Mass, sat in the back corner, and left as soon as Mass was over, rarely speaking to anyone.

During the first group sessions, she sat slumped in her chair, her posture saying, "Don't notice me." Each week as we discussed our talents, she seemed to sit up straighter. By the fourth session, she was sitting completely straight up, and in that session, she finally spoke. She said, "God gave me these talents, and with my passion for helping people, I have what it takes to be a pastoral care minister. This is something I really want. What do I have to do to be part of this ministry?"

We witnessed God's glory that evening in the life of one of our parishioners. I know her life has changed, and ours certainly did too!

Marie Guido
Port Jefferson Station, New York, United States

Expressing All of Her Talents

Deb, a woman in a group I worked with had a hard time getting along with others. She was adamant about her opinions, and she was very vocal. The group was often on edge when she was in the room because they didn't want to trigger a confrontation.

Well, we were amazed to learn that Empathy is Deb's top theme. Her coaching session seemed to change everything. She realized that her need to express her opinions was driven by her powerful Maximizer talents — and possibly most importantly that her Empathy talents also held great value.

As weeks went by, the tension went away. Deb continued to articulate her observations about opportunities for improvement, but she shared them in ways that showed she was tuned in to the other group members. Each week when she walked in, you could immediately see the difference. She seemed to light up; her appearance changed; she carried herself differently; and she smiled all of the time. She was free. She is now a much more effective Maximizer because she has learned to express all of her talents. The discovery of one's greatest talents brings hope and fulfillment to the lives of people who desperately need it.

Kristy McAdams
Lutz, Florida, United States

What a Relief!

Rose and her husband have been part of the leadership team for a number of years. A couple of years ago, Rose told us she felt she no longer had much to contribute, and she stood down from the role. At the time, she still participated in the children's ministry but struggled with that as well.

As a mother to four children, ages 6 to 13, and a part-time kindergarten teacher, Rose leads a busy life. She is very organized and gives 100% to everything she does.

When we sat down to discuss Rose's talents, she thought I was trying to get her more involved. She was very relieved when I told her that was not my intention. She was even more relieved when we discussed the likelihood that her talents would usually cause her to function better when doing *fewer* things. Her combination of top themes meant that anyone or anything she committed herself to would get her full attention. She does nothing haphazardly and loves to see results in people and any task she takes on.

Rose is now far more relaxed about her various roles, especially her role in the church. She contributes in ways that make the best use of her greatest talents, and she makes a strong impact. She also feels much more supported in her kindergarten work (in fact, a ministry to families). In addition, this understanding of her talents has had a positive impact on her marriage. The tension that existed between her and her husband about the conflict between church commitments and family life has been reduced significantly, and this improvement enables both to enjoy using their talents in the areas they consider most important.

Rob Nicholls
Box Hill South, Victoria, Australia

A Very Good Development

Pamela is retired. Her husband passed away several months ago. As she has grieved his loss, Pamela has been trying to identify a ministry to pursue.

Pamela's five Signature Themes are Developer, Input, Learner, Empathy, and Connectedness. When she first saw her top themes, Pamela seriously doubted that she truly was a Developer. However, as we talked, she told me about her career, in which she works as the office assistant in a school counselor's office. We discussed how she had always been able to see the good in young people and the possibilities in their lives. The more she reflected on her experiences, the clearer it became to her that she had, indeed, used her Developer talents consistently throughout her career.

After praying in search of God's guidance in selecting a ministry for this phase of her life, she is now seeking to become a mentor to elementary-aged school children. God has renewed His calling for Pamela to believe in and develop the hearts of children.

Kevin Hopkins
Choctaw, Oklahoma, United States

CHAPTER 6

Discovering a Calling

When we think of a "calling," we usually imagine the voice of God coming in the night. We also think that people who are called are somehow special — unusually devout — and not "regular folks" like us. Our view is reflected in the call of Samuel, found in the Old Testament:

> *During the time young Samuel was minister to the LORD under Eli, a revelation of the LORD was uncommon and vision infrequent. One day Eli was asleep in his usual place. His eyes had lately grown so weak that he could not see. The lamp of God was not yet extinguished, and Samuel was sleeping in the temple of the LORD where the ark of God was. The LORD called to Samuel, who answered, "Here I am." He ran to Eli and said, "Here I am. You called me." "I did not call you," Eli said. "Go back to sleep." So he went back to sleep.*
> 1 Samuel 3:1-5

Notice that Samuel didn't recognize the voice of God at first — he thought it was his mentor, Eli. But after three times (and some coaching from Eli), Samuel did recognize God's voice, responded to that call, and went on to become one of Israel's greatest prophets.

But callings aren't just for the devout and holy. Everyone has a calling. You just need to discover what it is. And that calling doesn't come from God's voice thundering from above; it comes from His whispers deep within you, from the very essence of your being. God expects nothing more from you than to live that life for which you were created. *He wants you to be yourself.*

When you discover your talents, you begin to discover your calling. When you build and apply strengths by making the most of your greatest talents, you fulfill your calling. Now, what do you think your calling might be? Take some time to reflect on the following:

- Dare to dream. If time and money were no object, what would you do for God?

- Where is your passion? What do you love to do?

- What are your greatest talents? How could you combine your talents and your passions to fulfill your calling?

- Talk to your pastor, your small-group leader, or someone in your parish who understands strengths-based organizations. Make a plan to explore the possibilities of combining your talents and your passions to fulfill your calling. It doesn't have to be in the parish; individuals' callings may lead them to such ministries as Habitat for Humanity, adult literacy projects, medical clinics for the poor, or Meals on Wheels — the possibilities are limitless. So are society's needs.

THE POWER OF BEING CALLED

Throughout the Bible, we see how people were called according to their talents to further God's vision for humankind. There was Abraham, who at the age of 75 had the courage to trust God and leave everything he had ever known to go to a place he had never seen. Relying on his talent for envisioning the future that God had promised him, he strategically forged alliances with foreign rulers to make his way as he lived in the new land.

There was Deborah, one of the judges of ancient Israel, who commanded respect and loyalty from the generals of the Israelite army. Her positivity inspired confidence in her followers in the face of overwhelming odds, and the song she sang of God's deliverance (one of the oldest portions of the Old Testament) celebrated her people's victory.

In the New Testament, when Jesus was first beginning his ministry, he walked by the Sea of Galilee and called his disciples. Each of them was uniquely created; each had a unique combination of talents. They were fishermen, government workers, businessmen, and students — "regular folks" like us.

Ever the activator, Peter was impetuous, ready to jump in without thinking things completely through — a man of action totally devoted to Jesus. Yet even when he made the greatest mistake of his life (denying that he ever knew Jesus), he recovered, found forgiveness, and tapped into those qualities that Jesus first saw in him — and became the leader of the new faith.

Thomas was cautious, analytical, always raising questions. And once he got the answers, he made known the strength of his conviction. Even when his demand for evidence of the Resurrection earned him the nickname "doubting Thomas," once he had his proof, he went on to eventually die for the Lord he loved.

Andrew was a fisherman, and after he was called, he was always looking for people to bring to Jesus so they too could have their lives changed. Andrew's talent for winning others over, his Woo, caused him to introduce his brother to Jesus — his brother Peter.

In so many ways, you are no different from the ordinary people with extraordinary talents who populate the Bible. Just like them, you too can find your calling. When you discover your talents and link those talents with your passion, there is no telling what God can accomplish through you.

God has created the one and only you, uniquely gifted with undeniable talents that are the foundation for your strengths. Claim who you are, listen to God, celebrate your talents, begin living through strengths. And start transforming your life — and the life of your parish.

The Clifton StrengthsFinder®: Research FAQs

March 2005

Submitted by:

Gallup, Inc.
1001 Gallup Drive
Omaha, Nebraska 68102

COPYRIGHT STANDARDS

FOREWORD

Many technical issues must be considered in the evaluation of an instrument such as the Clifton StrengthsFinder. One set of issues revolves around information technology and the expanding possibilities that Web-based applications offer for those who study human nature. Another set of issues involves what is known as psychometrics, which is the scientific study of human behavior through measurement. The Clifton StrengthsFinder is required to meet many American and international standards for psychometrics applied to test development (such as AERA/APA/NCME, 1999). The Clifton StrengthsFinder Research FAQs deal with some questions that emerge from those standards as well as technical questions that a leader may have about the use of the Clifton StrengthsFinder in his or her organization.

A few technical references have been cited for readers who wish to review primary source material. These technical materials may be found in local university libraries or on the Internet. The reader is encouraged to review the sources cited at the end of the FAQs. Readers with other research questions are encouraged to contact Gallup and request a copy of *The Clifton StrengthsFinder Technical Report: Development and Validation* (Lopez, Hodges, & Harter, 2005).

WHAT IS THE CLIFTON STRENGTHSFINDER?

The Clifton StrengthsFinder is a Web-based talent assessment instrument from the perspective of Strengths Psychology. Through a secure connection, the Clifton StrengthsFinder presents 180 items to the user. Each item lists a pair of potential self-descriptors, such as "I read instructions

233

carefully" and "I like to jump right into things." The descriptors are placed as if anchoring polar ends of a continuum. From each pair, the participant is then asked to choose the descriptor that best describes him or her, and also the extent to which it does so. The participant is given 20 seconds to respond to a given item before the system moves on to the next item. (Clifton StrengthsFinder developmental research showed that the 20-second limit resulted in a negligible item noncompletion rate.)

IS THE CLIFTON STRENGTHSFINDER SUPPOSED TO BE A WORK-RELATED INVENTORY, A CLINICAL INVENTORY, BOTH, OR NEITHER?

The Clifton StrengthsFinder is an omnibus assessment based on Strengths Psychology. Its primary application has been in the work domain, but it has been used for understanding individuals in a variety of roles and settings — employees, executive teams, students, families, and personal development. It is *not* intended for clinical assessment or diagnosis of psychiatric disorders.

WHY ISN'T THE CLIFTON STRENGTHSFINDER BASED ON THE "BIG FIVE" FACTORS OF PERSONALITY THAT HAVE BEEN WELL ESTABLISHED IN RESEARCH JOURNALS SINCE THE 1980'S?

The "big five" factors of personality are neuroticism (which reflects emotional stability — reverse-scored), extroversion (seeking the company of others), openness (interest in new experiences, ideas, and so forth), agreeableness (likeability, harmoniousness), and conscientiousness (rule abidance, discipline, integrity). A substantial amount of scientific research has demonstrated that human personality functioning can be summarized in terms of these five dimensions. This research has been conducted across cultures and languages (for example, McCrae and Costa, 1987; McCrae, Costa, Lima, et al., 1999; McCrae, Costa, Ostendorf, et al., 2000).

The major reason that the Clifton StrengthsFinder is not based on the big five is that the big five is a measurement model rather than a conceptual one. It was derived from factor analysis. No theory underpinned it. It consists of the most generally agreed upon minimal number of personality factors, but conceptually it is no more correct than a model with four or six factors (Block, 1995; Hogan, Hogan, and Roberts, 1996). Some parts of the Clifton StrengthsFinder could be boiled down to aspects of the big five, but nothing would be gained from doing so. In fact, reducing the respondent's Clifton StrengthsFinder score to five dimensions would produce less information than is produced by any current measure of the big five, as those measures report subscores within those of the five major dimensions.

HOW WAS THE CLIFTON STRENGTHSFINDER DEVELOPED?

The conceptual basis of the Clifton StrengthsFinder is grounded in more than three decades of the study of success across a wide variety of functions in business and education. Data from more than two million individuals were considered in the development of the Clifton StrengthsFinder. The item pairs were selected from a database of criterion-related validity studies, including more than 100 predictive validity studies (Schmidt & Rader, 1999). Factor and reliability analyses were conducted in multiple samples to assess the contribution of items to measurement of themes and the consistency and stability of theme scores — thereby achieving the goal of a balance between maximized theme information and efficiency in instrument length.

WHY DOES THE CLIFTON STRENGTHSFINDER USE THESE 180 ITEM PAIRS AND NOT OTHERS?

These pairs reflect Gallup's research over three decades of studying successful people in a systematic, structured manner. They were derived from a quantitative review of item functioning, from a content review of the representativeness of themes and items within themes, with an eye toward the construct validity of the entire assessment. Given the breadth of talent we wish to assess, the pool of items is large and diverse. Well-known personality assessments range from 150 to upward of 400 items.

ARE THE CLIFTON STRENGTHSFINDER ITEMS IPSATIVELY SCORED, AND IF SO, DOES THIS LIMIT SCORING OF THE ITEMS?

Ipsativity is a mathematical term that refers to an aspect of a data matrix, such as a set of scores. A data matrix is said to be ipsative when the sum of the scores for each respondent is a constant. More generally, ipsativity refers to a set of scores that define a person in particular but is comparable between persons in only a very limited way. For example, if you rank-ordered your favorite colors and someone else rank-ordered their favorite colors, one could not compare the *intensity* of preference for any particular color due to ipsativity; only the *ranking* could be compared. Of the 180 Clifton StrengthsFinder items, less than 30 percent are ipsatively scored. These items are distributed over the range of Clifton StrengthsFinder themes, and no one theme contains more than one item scored in a way that would produce an ipsative data matrix (Plake, 1999).

HOW ARE CLIFTON STRENGTHSFINDER THEME SCORES CALCULATED?

Scores are calculated on the basis of the mean of the intensity of self-description. The respondent is given three response options for each self-description: strongly agree, agree, and neutral. A proprietary formula assigns a value to each response category. Values for items in the theme are averaged to derive a theme score. Scores can be reported as a mean, as a standard score, or as a percentile.

WAS MODERN TEST SCORE THEORY (FOR EXAMPLE, IRT) USED TO DEVELOP THE CLIFTON STRENGTHSFINDER?

The Clifton StrengthsFinder was developed to capitalize on the accumulated knowledge and experience of Gallup's strengths-based development practice. Thus, items were initially chosen on the basis of traditional validity evidence (construct, content, criterion). This is a universally accepted method for developing assessments. Methods to apply IRT to assessments that are both heterogeneous and homogeneous are only now being explored (for example, Waller, Thompson, and Wenk, 2000). Further iterations of the Clifton StrengthsFinder may well use other statistical methods to refine the instrument.

WHAT CONSTRUCT VALIDITY RESEARCH HAS BEEN CONDUCTED IN RELATION TO THE CLIFTON STRENGTHSFINDER?

The Clifton StrengthsFinder is an omnibus assessment of talents based on Strengths Psychology. Therefore, it undoubtedly has correlational linkages to these measures to about the same extent that personality measures link to other measures in general.

Construct validity can be assessed through a number of analysis types. During development phases, a number of items were pilot tested. The items with the strongest psychometric properties (including item correlation to theme) were retained.

Items should correlate to their proposed themes (constructs) at a higher level than they do to other themes (constructs.) In a follow-up study of 601,049 respondents, the average item-to-proposed-theme correlation (corrected for part-whole overlap) was 6.6 times larger than the average item correlation to other themes.

Construct validity can also be assessed on the basis of convergent and discriminant validity evidence. A 2003 construct validity study explored the relationship between the Clifton StrengthsFinder and the five-factor model of personality. Several expected associations between Clifton StrengthsFinder themes and five-factor model constructs were found. For example, the Discipline theme correlates .81 with a measure of conscientiousness. Theoretically, these constructs have similar definition in relation to orderliness and planning. Other examples include the .83 correlation between Woo and extroversion, the .70 correlation between Ideation and intellectence, and the .58 correlation between Positivity and agreeableness.

Convergent and discriminant validity studies are a part of past and ongoing construct validity research.

CAN CLIFTON STRENGTHSFINDER SCORES CHANGE?

This is an important question for which there are both technical and conceptual answers.

Technical answers: The talents measured by Clifton StrengthsFinder are expected to demonstrate a property called reliability. Reliability has several definitions. The most important form of reliability estimate for the Clifton StrengthsFinder is technically known as test-retest reliability, which is the extent to which scores are stable over time. Test-retest reliabilities on the Clifton StrengthsFinder themes are high in relation to current psychometric standards.

Almost all Clifton StrengthsFinder themes have a test-retest reliability over a six-month interval between .60 and .80. A maximum test-retest reliability score of 1 would indicate that all Clifton StrengthsFinder respondents received *exactly* the same score over two assessments. The average correlation of an individual's theme ranking across multiple time periods is .74 (across 706 participants with an average of 17 months between administrations).

Conceptual answers: While an evaluation of the full extent of this stability is, of course, an empirical question, the conceptual origins of a person's talents are also relevant. Gallup has studied the life themes of top performers in an extensive series of research studies combining qualitative and quantitative investigations over many years. Participants have ranged from youths in their early teens to adults in their mid-seventies. In each of these studies, the focal point was the identification of long-standing patterns of thought, feeling, and behavior associated with success. The lines of interview questioning used were both prospective and retrospective, such as "What do you want to be doing ten years from now?" and "At what age did you make your first sale?" In other words, the timeframe of interest in our original studies of excellence in job performance was long term, not short term. Many of the items developed provided useful predictions of job stability, thereby suggesting that the measured attributes were of a persistent nature. Tracking studies of job performance over two- to three-year time spans added to the Gallup understanding of what it takes for a job incumbent to be consistently effective, rather than just achieve impressive short-term gains. The prominence of dimensions and items relating to motivation and to values in much of the original life themes research also informed the design of a Clifton StrengthsFinder instrument that can identify those enduring human qualities.

At this relatively early stage in the application of the Clifton StrengthsFinder, it is not yet clear how long an individual's salient features, so measured, will endure. In general, however, it is likely to be years rather than months. We may perhaps project a minimum of five years and upper ranges of 30 to 40 years and longer. There is growing evidence (for example, Judge, Higgins, Thoresen, and Barrick, 1999) that some aspects of personality are predictive throughout many decades of the life span. Some Clifton StrengthsFinder themes may turn out to be more enduring than others. Cross-sectional studies of different age groups will provide the earliest insights into possible age-related changes in normative patterns of behaviors. The first explanations for apparent changes in themes, as measured, should therefore be sought in the direction of measurement error rather than as indications of a true change in the underlying trait, emotion, or cognition. The respondents themselves should also be invited to offer an explanation for any apparent discrepancies.

HOW CAN ONE DETERMINE THAT THE CLIFTON STRENGTHSFINDER WORKS?

The question of whether an assessment such as the Clifton StrengthsFinder "works" is addressed in an ongoing study of the construct validity of the instrument through psychometric and conceptual review. The Clifton StrengthsFinder is based on more than 30 years of evidence as to the nature of talents and the application of strengths analysis. This evidence was summarized in a recent scientific study that used meta-analysis (Schmidt & Rader, 1999).

The research literature in the behavioral and social sciences includes a multitude of individual studies with apparently conflicting conclusions. Meta-analysis allows the researcher to estimate the mean correlation between variables and make corrections for artifactual sources of variation in findings across studies. As such, it provides uniquely powerful information because it controls for measurement and sampling errors and other idiosyncrasies that distort the results of individual studies. (More than one thousand meta-analyses have been published in the psychological, educational, behavioral, medical, and personnel selection fields.) For a detailed review of meta-analysis across a variety of fields, see Lipsey and Wilson (1993).

WHAT IS STRENGTHS-BASED DEVELOPMENT?

Strengths-based development is a process that leads to an individual's ability to consistently perform a specific task at a nearly perfect level. A strength is made up of skills, knowledge, and talents. Skills are one's basic abilities to perform the steps of specific tasks, such as the ability to operate a computer. Skills do not naturally exist within us; they must be acquired through training and practice. Knowledge, defined simply as what you know, includes facts (factual knowledge) and understandings (gained through experience) that can be productively applied to specific tasks. Knowledge does not naturally exist within us; it must be acquired. Talents are recurring patterns of thought, feeling, or behavior that can be productively applied to specific tasks, such as the inner drive to compete, sensitivity to the needs of others, and the tendency to be outgoing at social gatherings. Although talents cannot be acquired, we each have talents that naturally exist within us — and because those talents represent the best of our natural selves, they are the crucial component of strengths and our best opportunities to perform at levels of excellence.

Identification of talent is critical to strengths-based development. A popular means of identifying talent is to consider an individual's top five areas of talent as indicated by responses to the Clifton StrengthsFinder, Gallup's online talent assessment instrument. Considering these top five areas ("themes") of talent, known as one's Signature Themes, can help individuals understand and, as a result, internalize the themes that offer their most natural talents.

Signature Themes are a useful resource in the identification of talent. One's spontaneous reactions to any situation are an important indicator of talents, and the ranking of themes presented in a Clifton StrengthsFinder report is based upon spontaneous, top-of-mind reactions to the paired descriptors presented by the instrument.

Yearnings, rapid learning, satisfactions, and timelessness should also be considered when identifying talents (Clifton & Nelson, 1992). Yearnings reveal the presence of a talent, particularly when they are felt early in life. A yearning can be described as a pull, a magnetic influence, which draws one to a particular activity or environment time and again. Rapid learning offers another trace of talent. In the context of a new challenge or a new environment, something sparks in individual's talent. Immediately their brain seems to light up as if a whole bank of switches were suddenly flicked to "on" — and the speed at which they learn a new skill or gain new knowledge provides a telltale clue to the talent's presence and power. Satisfactions are psychological fulfillment that results when one takes on and successfully meets challenges that engage their greatest talents. Timelessness can also serve as a clue to talent. When individuals become so engrossed in an activity that they lose track of time, it may be because the activity engaged one of their talents.

Strengths-based development begins with the identification of talent, and continues as one integrates his or her talents into his or her view of self. Successful strengths-based development results in desired behavioral change (Clifton & Harter, 2003). Client-sponsored studies have provided evidence that strengths-based development relates to various positive outcomes, including increases in employee engagement and productivity.

Managers who create environments in which employees are able to make the most of their talents have more productive work units with less employee turnover (Clifton & Harter, 2003). Studies show that strengths-based development increases self-confidence, direction, hope, and altruism (Hodges & Clifton, 2004). Ongoing research continues to explore the impact of strengths-based development on desired outcomes.

HOW CAN THE CLIFTON STRENGTHSFINDER BE ADMINISTERED, SCORED, AND REPORTED FOR INDIVIDUALS WHO ARE UNABLE TO USE THE INTERNET BECAUSE OF EITHER DISABILITY OR ECONOMIC STATUS?

In regard to economic status (a.k.a. the digital divide), possible solutions include accessing the Internet from a library or school. It should be noted that some organizations with which Gallup works do not have universal Internet access. In these cases, as with those from disadvantaged backgrounds, the solution generally has involved special access from a few central locations.

In regard to disability, a range of accommodations is available. Generally, the most effective is for the participant to request that the timer that governs the pace of the Clifton StrengthsFinder administration be turned off. This and other accommodations would need to be arranged with Gallup on a case-by-case basis in advance of taking the Clifton StrengthsFinder.

WHAT IS THE RECOMMENDED READING LEVEL FOR CLIFTON STRENGTHSFINDER USERS? WHAT ALTERNATIVES ARE AVAILABLE FOR THOSE WHO DO NOT MEET THAT LEVEL?

The Clifton StrengthsFinder is designed for completion by those with at least an eighth- to tenth-grade reading level (in most cases, those 14 years of age or older). Trials of the Clifton StrengthsFinder in our youth leadership studies have demonstrated neither significant nor consistent problems in completion of the Clifton StrengthsFinder by teens. Possible alternatives or accommodations include turning off the pace timer to allow time to consult a dictionary or otherwise seek the meaning of a word.

IS THE CLIFTON STRENGTHSFINDER APPROPRIATE ACROSS DEMOGRAPHIC GROUPS, COUNTRIES, AND LANGUAGES?

There is overwhelming evidence from both Gallup and other research organizations that the structure of talent and personality dimensions such as those measured by the Clifton StrengthsFinder and other instruments does not vary across cultures and nationalities.

For instance, the average item-to-theme correlation is quite similar across countries. The standard deviation of the correlations across countries is .026 and ranges from .01 to .04 across themes. Across languages, similar results were obtained, with an average standard deviation of the correlations across languages of .024 and range from .01 to .03. With regard to theme intercorrelations, the standard deviation across countries averaged .03 with range of .01 to .07 across the 561 theme intercorrelations. Across languages, the standard deviation averaged .02, with range from .01 to .06. In summary, the theme intercorrelations are stable across cultural contexts.

The Clifton StrengthsFinder has international presence as a talent measurement instrument. At this time (January 2008) it is available in 22 languages, with several other translations planned for the future. More than 110,000 of the first one million respondents completed the Clifton StrengthsFinder in a language other than English. Clifton StrengthsFinder respondents have come from more than 50 countries. More than 30 of these countries have had at least 1,000 respondents. Well over 600,000 respondents report a country of residence other than the United States.

Research exploring the age of Clifton StrengthsFinder respondents has revealed that the average item-to-theme correlation is quite similar across age groups. Average standard deviation of the correlations is .02 and ranges from .00 to .09 across themes.

Research into the gender of Clifton StrengthsFinder respondents has revealed that the item-total correlations are similar and consistently positive. Differences in item-total correlations between genders range from .00 to .06 across themes.

WHAT FEEDBACK DOES A RESPONDENT GET FROM THE CLIFTON STRENGTHSFINDER?

Feedback varies in accordance with the reason the person completes the Clifton StrengthsFinder. Sometimes the respondent receives only a report listing his or her top five themes — those in which the person received his or her highest scores. In other situations the person may also review the remaining 29 themes, along with action suggestions for each theme, in a personal feedback session with a Gallup consultant or in a supervised team-building session with their colleagues.

Theme combinations are rare and powerful. There are 278,256 possible unique combinations of Signature Themes, and 33.39 million different permutations with unique order can exist.

Since 1998, the Clifton StrengthsFinder has been used as Gallup's initial diagnostic tool in development programs with various academic institutions, faith-based organizations, major businesses, and other organizations. The Clifton StrengthsFinder has been used to facilitate the development of individuals across hundreds of roles including: manager, customer service representative, salesperson, administrative assistant, nurse, lawyer, pastor, leader, student, teacher, and school administrator.

REFERENCES FOR THE CLIFTON STRENGTHSFINDER RESEARCH FAQS

The following references are provided for readers interested in particular details of these FAQs. This reference list is not meant to be exhaustive, and although many of the references use advanced statistical techniques, the reader should not be deterred from reviewing them.

American Educational Research Association, American Psychological Association, National Council on Measurement in Education (AERA/APA/NCME). 1999. *Standards for educational and psychological testing.* Washington, D.C.: American Educational Research Association.

American Psychologist. Positive psychology [special issue]. 2000. Washington, D.C.: American Psychological Association.

Block, J. 1995. A contrarian view of the five-factor approach to personality description. *Psychological Bulletin* 117:187–215.

Cameron, K.S., Dutton, J.E., & Quinn, R.E. (Eds.). 2003. *Positive organizational scholarship.* San Francisco: Berrett-Koehler.

Clifton, D.O., & Harter, J.K. 2003. Strengths investment. In K.S. Cameron, J.E. Dutton, & R.E. Quinn (Eds.), *Positive organizational scholarship.* (pp. 111-121). San Francisco: Berrett-Koehler.

Clifton, D.O, & Nelson, P. 1992. Soar with your strengths. New York: Delacorte Press.

Clifton, J.K. 2002. Letter addressed to attendees of the first international Positive Psychology Summit, Washington, DC.

Hodges, T.D., & Clifton, D.O. 2004. Strengths-based development in practice. In A. Linley & S. Joseph (Eds.), *Handbook of positive psychology in practice.* Hoboken, New Jersey: John Wiley and Sons, Inc.

Hogan, R., J. Hogan, and B. W. Roberts. 1996. Personality measurement and employment decisions: Questions and answers. *American Psychologist* 51:469–77.

Hunter, J. E., and F. L. Schmidt. 1990. *Methods of meta-analysis: Correcting error and bias in research findings.* Newbury Park, CA: Sage.

Judge, T. A., C. A. Higgins, C. J. Thoresen, and M. R. Barrick. 1999. The big five personality traits, general mental ability, and career success across the life span. *Personnel Psychology* 52:621–52.

Keyes, C.L.M., & Haidt, J. (Eds.). 2003. *Flourishing: Positive psychology and the life well-lived.* Washington, DC: APA.

Linley, A., & Joseph, S. (Eds.). 2004. *Positive psychology in practice.* Hoboken, NJ: John Wiley & Sons, Inc.

Lipsey, M. W., and D. B. Wilson. 1993. The efficacy of psychological, educational, and behavioral treatment. *American Psychologist* 48:1181–1209.

Lopez, S.J., Hodges, T.D., and Harter, J.K. 2005. The Clifton Strengths-Finder technical report: Development and validation. Princeton, NJ: Gallup.

Lopez, S.J., & Snyder, C.R. (Eds.). 2003. *Positive psychological assessment: A handbook of models and measures.* Washington, DC: American Psychological Association.

McCrae, R. R., and P. T. Costa. 1987. Validation of the five-factor model of personality across instruments and observers. *Journal of Personality and Social Psychology* 52:81–90.

McCrae, R. R., P. T. Costa, M. P. de Lima, et al. 1999. Age differences in personality across the adult life span: Parallels in five cultures. *Developmental Psychology* 35:466–77.

McCrae, R. R., P. T. Costa, F. Ostendorf, et al. 2000. Nature over nurture: Temperament, personality, and life span development. *Journal of Personality and Social Psychology* 78:173–86.

Myers, D. 2000. The funds, friends, and faith of happy people. *American Psychologist*, 55: 56-67.

Plake, B. 1999. *An investigation of ipsativity and multicollinearity properties of the StrengthsFinder Instrument* [technical report]. Lincoln, NE: Gallup.

Schmidt, F.L., & Rader, M. 1999. Exploring the boundary conditions for interview validity: Meta-analytic validity findings for a new interview type. *Personnel Psychology*, 52: 445-464.

Sheldon, K., Fredrickson, B., Rathunde, K., & Csikszentmihalyi, M. 2000. Positive psychology manifesto (Rev. Ed.). Philadelphia. Retrieved May 1, 2003 from the World Wide Web: http://www.positivepsychology.org/akumalmanifesto.htm.

Snyder, C.R., & Lopez, S.J. (Eds.). 2002. *The handbook of positive psychology*. New York: Oxford University Press.

Waller, N. G., J. S. Thompson, and E. Wenk. 2000. Using IRT to separate measurement bias from true group differences on homogeneous and heterogeneous scales: An illustration with the MMPI. *Psychological Methods* 5:125–46.

ACKNOWLEDGEMENTS

There are so many individuals who helped make this book a reality, and we owe them a great debt of gratitude.

Many thanks to Jim Clifton, Gallup's chairman and CEO, whose vision of influencing every single world leader with Gallup's discoveries led to the creation of the Faith Communities Practice. Without his commitment to that vision, this book would never have happened.

Thank you to Larry Emond and Evan Perkins for their support, encouragement, and insight; to Geoff Brewer, one of the most talented editors on the planet; to the editing team of Paul Petters, Mark Stiemann, and Kelly Henry, whose talents for attention to detail were invaluable. Dennis Welch, Scott Simmons, and Cinda Hicks helped us keep the needs of the market clearly in mind. Tom Rath and Piotrek Juszkiewicz were superb managers and always made sure that the project was on track and on schedule. Chin-Yee Lai designed the book's excellent and compelling cover, and Kim Simeon, Mary Gansemer, and Molly Hardin produced the attractive and easy-to-read layout.

A host of other Gallup associates also made significant contributions to the *Living Your Strengths* project. They include Sherry Ehrlich, Irene Burklund, Wyn Wadginski, Lori Stohs, Jerry Krueger, Kryste Wiedenfeld, Rosemary Travis, Jim Harter, Tim Hodges, Julie Hawkins, Sue Munn, Tonya Fredstrom, and Robyn Seals.

Finally and most importantly, we express our deepest gratitude to our wives, Jane Winseman, Shirley Clifton, and Rosanne Liesveld, and our children, who supported and encouraged us throughout the process.

For more information about how to put the power of *Living Your Strengths* to work in your church, please call 212.899.4709.

If you'd like to contact us via e-mail, or share with us how your parish is making the most of its strengths, please contact us at lys@gallup.com.

Gallup Press exists to educate and inform the people who govern, manage, teach, and lead the world's six billion citizens. Each book meets Gallup's requirements of integrity, trust, and independence and is based on Gallup-approved science and research.